THE LIMITS OF RELIGIOUS TOLERANCE

THE LIMITS OF RELIGIOUS TOLERANCE

Alan Jay Levinovitz

Public Works

AUSTIN D. SARAT *Series Editor*

Conceived as a "digital pamphlet" series, titles in *Public Works* seek out and make available to a wide audience of readers the perspectives of leading scholars in the humanities on questions rising to significance in our public conversation, and demanding more discerning examination and penetrating insight. Shorter than monographs, these works offer both authors and readers the freedom of long-form essays and the tools of digital media to see through the lens of the human experience the seemingly intractable questions confronting a complex, deeply interconnected, and sometimes shockingly violent world.

Essays published in *Public Works* series are available as open-access works of scholarship, immediately and freely available to readers and thinkers everywhere. As digital works, they will be published to the web and also downloadable to a variety of reading devices.

THE LIMITS OF RELIGIOUS TOLERANCE

Published by The Amherst College Press
Robert Frost Library • Amherst, Massachusetts

ISBN 978-1-943208-04-3 paperback
ISBN 978-1-943208-05-0 electronic book

Library of Congress Control Number: 2016956792

Table of Contents

Acknowledgments

I am indebted to the extensive and thoughtful comments of my editor and two anonymous reviewers.

To believers everywhere, with all due respect

"A person who thinks only about building walls, wherever they may be, and not building bridges, is not Christian."

—Pope Francis, in answer to a question about Donald Trump

"For a religious leader to question a person's faith is disgraceful. No leader, especially a religious leader, should have the right to question another man's religion or faith."

—Donald Trump's response to the pope*

---

* Alan Rappaport, "Donald Trump Calls Pope's Criticism 'Disgraceful'," *New York Times*, February 18, 2016, http://www.nytimes.com/politics/first-draft/2016/02/18/donald-trump-calls-popes-criticism-disgraceful/

Introduction

In early 2014, a student named Daniel Harper started passing out fly-ers at Cameron University in Oklahoma. The flyers outlined Harper's extensive and damning objections to a religious group active on cam-pus, the World Mission Society. As an evangelical Christian, Harper felt he needed to inform fellow students that the WMS was a danger-ous cult that used "mind control" techniques to brainwash members, and that WMS Bible study sessions offered a view of scripture that would "twist and bend" its meaning.[1]

A publicly funded school, Cameron University had in place a speech code that barred "offensive" and "discriminatory" speech. Other stu-dents, offended by the flyers, filed a complaint; and university admin-istrators eventually decided against Harper. The flyers, they wrote in their decision letter, had been "specifically created to denounce anoth-er person's religious beliefs." Public distribution of the flyers there-fore constituted "discrimination based on religion," in violation of the campus code. Harper was instructed to be "respectful" of other peo-ple's religious beliefs. Refusal to do so threatened "the basic values of religious freedom [that] are provided to every citizen of our country," along with the "educational mission" of the university. In short, Harp-er was being religiously intolerant, and his intolerance was not to be tolerated.

According to a 2016 report by the Foundation for Individual Rights in Education (FIRE), about half of America's campuses maintain speech codes like Cameron University's, policies FIRE characterizes as

---

1. For coverage of the incident and links to primary documents see
Susan Kruth, "Cameron U. Sued After Prohibiting Student from
Distributing Flyers," TheFire.org, May 23, 2014, https://www.thefire.org/
cameron-u-sued-after-prohibiting-student-from-distributing-flyers/.

"clearly and substantially prohibit[ing] protected speech."[2] The codes often contain vague terms such as "verbal abuse" or "discriminatory speech," the prohibition of which is meant to foster an atmosphere of mutual respect and tolerance. Though enacted by administrations, they are often drafted at the behest of students, who are increasingly supportive of measures that allow for the banning of "extreme" speakers and offensive speech on campuses.[3]

Thanks to recent high-profile incidents at Wesleyan, Yale, Northwestern, and Georgetown Law School, these codes are now receiving wide coverage in popular media. The resulting public debates touch on a range of thorny philosophical questions. What is "tolerance"? Under what conditions should we be tolerant? What does it mean to say someone doesn't have the "right" to be intolerant? Answers to these questions tend to be poorly articulated, vague, and different from one discussion to the next. People have the legal *right* to say all manner of intolerant things; but the law, presumably, is not Donald Trump's concern when says, "No leader, especially a religious leader, should have the right to question another man's religion or faith." If not the law, then what normative standard should advocates of tolerance and respect appeal to? Does the same standard apply on campuses and in public parks?

Normative standards can differ from legal standards, and it is the former, with regards to tolerance and intolerance, that will be the focus of this essay. The central question is not whether and under what circumstances citizens have a legal right to proselytize publicly or denounce other faiths. The United States Supreme Court's unanimous decision in *Cantwell v. Smith* (1940)—which concerned the right of Jehovah's Witnesses to proselytize using anti-Catholic material in a Roman Catholic neighborhood—set a precedent for protecting potentially incendiary religious claims in a public forum from charges of disturbing the peace. Nevertheless, just because an action is legally protected does not mean one ought to perform it (and vice versa).

---

2. "Spotlight on speech codes 2016: The state of free speech on our nation's campuses," thefire.org, https://www.thefire.org/spotlight-on-speech-codes-2016/.

3. 2015 data can be found in the Higher Education Research Institute's report: http://www.heri.ucla.edu.

Most cases of everyday religious tolerance or intolerance fall into the category of legally permissible actions that may not be advisable—or conducive to the conditions of democratic order.

This essay argues that in order to answer questions about the advisability of tolerance, legal or otherwise, we must first be clearer about what tolerance means. Too often, tolerance is confused with such virtues as respect or kindness, which in turn makes it seem as though one cannot be intolerant without also being unkind and disrespectful. Against that position, I defend the counterintuitive claim that one can indeed be intolerant while also being kind and respectful—in fact, respect for others as rational persons who desire to hold true beliefs may, in certain circumstances, actually permit, indeed demand, intolerance.

I examine the implications of this alternative understanding of intolerance by focusing on religiously intolerant beliefs and language of the sort exemplified in Daniel Harper's flyer—or in Thomas Jefferson's judgment that the last book of the New Testament is "merely the ravings of a maniac, no more worthy, nor capable of explanation than the incoherences of our own nightly dreams."[4] That is, I focus on public speech meant to denounce certain (or all) religious beliefs. Of course there are significant differences between intolerance based on religion and intolerance based on race, gender, or sexual preference. Calling the World Mission Society a "dangerous cult" is not the same thing as saying that homosexuality is unnatural and ought to be illegal. It is entirely possible that speech asserting the former should be allowed on campuses while speech asserting the latter should not be.[5] Such issues are beyond the scope of this essay, but it is my hope that the following examination of the practical and philosophical issues attending religious tolerance might inform debates about the appropriate limits of tolerance more generally.[6]

---

4. Emrys Westacott, *The Virtues of Our Vices* (Princeton: Princeton University Press, 2011), 218.

5. On the other hand, one could also argue that religion "can be given and unchosen and in this respect it is similar to human characteristics such as ethnicity and gender." Commission on Religion and Belief in British Public Life, *Living with Difference: Community, Diversity, and the Common Good* (Cambridge: The Woolf Institute, 2015), 14.

6. If, as Brian Leiter suggests, religious beliefs deserve no more or less tolerance than any other kind of belief, the arguments presented here should apply to other forms of intolerance as well. I have some reservations about the transferability of his argument

Similarly, while the following discussion attempts to articulate a clear definition of tolerance applicable in all domains of belief and behavior, it would require far more space to pursue the implications of this definition across those domains. Instead, I focus on the limits of tolerance in spaces dedicated to higher education. It will become clear that debates about the limits of tolerance depend on context. Just as the law distinguishes between the privacy of one's own home and the public square, more general considerations must also recognize that intolerance can be advisable in some contexts and not others; on campus, perhaps, but not as a dinner host. Even campuses admit of further subdivisions—the classroom and the quadrangle, dorm rooms and restrooms. I do not expect to earn every readers' agreement on how intolerance should fit into these spaces. Rather, my hope is simply to exonerate intolerance from its current status as an unequivocal vice, and provide a model for rigorous and nuanced debate over its proper place, both in higher education and in the world.

I. Tolerance and Respect

Much like pornography, perhaps the most serious problem with debates about tolerance is a marked absence of terminological precision. Consider the 2015 "Statement of Principles Against Intolerance," drafted by the University of California system in response to frequent acrimonious protests about politics in the Middle East, as well as separate anti-Semitic incidents.

> We define intolerance as unwelcome conduct motivated by discrimination against, or hatred toward, other individuals or groups. It may take the form of acts of violence or intimidation, threats, harassment, hate speech, derogatory language reflecting stereotypes or prejudice, or inflammatory or derogatory use of culturally recognized symbols of hate, prejudice, or discrimination.[7]

---

from the legal sphere, where it seems to hold, into other spheres such as higher education, the one I consider here. Leiter, *Why Tolerate Religion?* (Princeton: Princeton University Press, 2014).

7. See coverage of the incidents in Josh Logue, "Defining Intolerance," *Inside Higher Ed*, March 16, 2016, https://www.insidehighered.com/news/2016/03/16/u-california-considers-revised-intolerance-policy. The statement itself can be accessed online from the

What does the document mean by "intolerance"? The problem here is that "unwelcome conduct" and "discrimination" are ambiguous concepts, admitting to a variety of meanings. Most problematically, it appears to be the case that disimpassioned statements of fact could easily be taken as reflecting a motivation of prejudice or hatred. It is hard to imagine a Scientologist who wouldn't understand the statement "Scientology is a cult" as "derogatory language" reflecting deeply held prejudice—perhaps rightfully so. Foreclosing on all "unwelcome conduct" and "derogatory language" creates the distinct possibility of suppressing a great deal of speech that ought to be allowed.

Another approach to defining tolerance reduces it to a kind of respect. In the "Statement of Principles Against Intolerance," we read that "tolerance...requires [that] University of California students, faculty, and staff must respect the dignity of each person within the UC community." So constructed, tolerance, whatever it means, is a consequence of our duty to respect other people's fundamental nature as human beings of intrinsic worth. This approach, which connects tolerance and respect for persons, appears frequently in scholarly literature. At the very least, goes the argument, we must tolerate others because we respect them as persons with autonomy, identities, and the right to self-determination. Respect for persons, as Susan Mendus writes, "both grounds and sets limits to toleration."[8] We tolerate all beliefs and behavior that are respectful of personhood, and we do not tolerate those that violate one's personhood.

Yet this approach is also problematic. Defining tolerance in terms of respect for persons empties tolerance of any content and makes it identical with the demands of one's basic moral philosophy. As Brian Leiter points out, respect for persons is "minimal respect," and makes "no substantive moral demand on action" beyond treating people as you think people ought to be treated.[9] This creates a paradox: If you are evangelical about your religious beliefs (or lack thereof), you may

---

Board of Regents website: http://regents.universityofcalifornia.edu/regmeet/sept15/e4.pdf

8. Susan Mendus, "Introduction," in *Justifying Toleration: Conceptual and Historical Perspectives* ed. Susan Mendus (Cambridge: Cambridge University Press, 2009), 12.

9. Leiter, *Why Tolerate Religion?*, 71.

believe it is disrespectful of someone's personhood to allow them to continue believing falsehoods. You may think that true autonomy happens only (say) when one is liberated through Jesus—or from Jesus. At the same time, being told that you are gravely mistaken about your religious beliefs can feel deeply disrespectful of your core personal identity—hence the difficulty with Harper's pamphlets.[10] Was Harper being disrespectful? Respect as respect for persons gives no real guidance on how to answer the question.

In *The Virtues of Our Vices*, Emrys Westacott attempts to solve this problem by distinguishing between various forms of respect. In addition to respect for persons, he identifies respect for a person's qualities, achievements, or accomplishments (what Leiter calls "appraisal respect"), respect for a person's right to hold a belief, and respect for a particular belief. The last of these is most relevant for the question of religious tolerance, and Westacott further subdivides respect for beliefs into six categories: epistemic, moral, historical, intellectual, aesthetic, and pragmatic. Westacott argues that although one might withhold "epistemic respect" from a religious belief, one can still respect the intellectual work that went into creating it, the beauty of its articulation, or the positive role it plays in people's lives—the afterlife as comfort in the face of a loved one's death, for example.

These are helpful distinctions because they allow for the possibility that, in certain significant ways, people can be respectful of religious beliefs while simultaneously denying their veracity. "Being willing to withhold respect from certain beliefs," writes Westacott, "is a corollary of critical thinking."[11] To assert that all religious beliefs deserve equal epistemic respect would be to endorse a strange form of uncritical relativism. His position allows us to reject relativism and still remain respectful.

Although this resolves some of the problems with respecting persons while rejecting the truth of their beliefs, it also highlights the difference between respect and tolerance. Many historians of science

---

10. See Peter Jones, "Beliefs and Identities," in *Toleration, Identity, and Difference*, ed. by John Horton and Susan Mendus (New York: St. Martin's Press, 1999), 67 and 72, for discussion of this tension.

11. Westacott, *The Virtues of Our Vices* , 205.

no doubt respect the intellectual work and beauty that went into the humoral theory of medicine. Yet these historians would not tolerate the teaching of humoral theory as fact in medical school. Intolerance is entirely compatible with some forms of respect, and the duty to respect persons and beliefs, however it plays out, does not map neatly onto related duties to be tolerant (or intolerant). Just because you respect a belief doesn't mean you should tolerate it. Nor does tolerance entail respect. If my friend told me that he firmly believes we should tolerate women in positions of power, I'd find his statement enormously disrespectful of women. The fact that he sees women as a presence to tolerate is, in itself, disrespectful of women as persons.

Distinguishing between tolerance and respect helps to avoid another potential mistake, namely the conflation of intolerance and incivility. Even when you think that other people's religious beliefs are erroneous or evil, civility requires that you express your thoughts politely, and, in certain contexts, refrain from expressing them at all. Intolerance is compatible with silence, and civility can demand it. If an athlete is being given an award in a public ceremony on campus, and she thanks god for her achievements, respect and civility dictate that one not shout, "God doesn't help people with sports!" The religiously intolerant may instead choose to write an opinion piece for the school newspaper, or, if they are so inclined, to approach the athlete in a different space and open a dialogue. Here, civil silence combines lack of respect for someone's belief with respect for her role—and the audience's role—in a public ceremony.

Unlike epistemic, moral, and aesthetic respect, civility is not merely an intellectual position. It is a behavior, which constitutes an entirely different type of respect. You can withhold all forms of intellectual respect from a belief—a crude conspiracy theory, for example—but that does not mean you can confront someone who believes in that theory and shout at her in the street. The same is true for religious beliefs. It is possible that the real problem with Harper's pamphlets, seen from the perspective of other students or of the institution's leaders, wasn't intolerance or intellectual disrespect, but rather incivility—the tone of the pamphlets and the forum in which they were presented.

Statements like the one issued by the University of California system tend to collapse or confuse the difference between different types of respect, as well as the relationship between respect and tolerance. Conflating all forms of respect and tolerance makes it seem as if intolerance of any kind necessarily violates respect for persons, unless one is being intolerant of basic violations of human rights. To withhold respect or to publically criticize someone's religious beliefs is to be unjustifiably intolerant, no matter what.

A serious drawback of this position is that it appears to prohibit public criticism of religious beliefs, which stifles intellectual freedom of the kind prized in liberal democratic societies and public institutions of higher education. For this reason, a 2015 report drafted by the Commission on Religion and Belief in British Life takes great pains to carve out space for public criticism within its vigorous defense of respect. Equal respect, states the report, does not "just mean toleration, in the sense of permitting."[12] Rather, equal respect goes beyond toleration, since "it involves the welcoming of difference and recognizes the identities that are important to their bearers."[13] The definition is quite strong, taking us beyond toleration of the sort required by minimal respect for persons. Nevertheless, the report assures readers that equal respect "is an attitude that can co-exist with vigorous disagreement and debate provided it is conducted on the basis that all are fellow citizens and in a spirit of civility."

Here, again, we see the difficulties that attend definitions of tolerance, respect, and civility. Tolerance is not respect. Respect requires citizens not only to permit, but also to "welcome" diverse religious beliefs—yet it also allows us to vigorously debate those religious beliefs, presumably because we believe that some of them are false, and because we hope that debate will eventually lead to the renouncement of those falsehoods. This last—the hope that through vigorous debate we can eliminate false religious beliefs—is motivated by intolerance of falsehoods. Suddenly we are faced with another paradox: respect

12. *Living with Difference: Community, Diversity, and the Common Good*, 25.

13. For a discussion of the difference between respect and "mere" toleration see Leiter, *Why Tolerate Religion?*, 69; and Martha C. Nussbaum, *Liberty of Conscience: In Defense of America's Tradition of Religious Equality* (New York: Basic Books, 2008), 19–25.

allows for the (civil) exercise of intolerance, yet respect also demands that we tolerate, indeed *welcome*, diverse religious beliefs, even those with which we disagree!

When tolerance is understood as a fundamental civic virtue, closely tied to respect, it is easy to see how a tolerant person would be extremely wary of publicly criticizing another's religion. Harmonizing tolerance and criticism is certainly possible, but as we have seen it requires complicated philosophical positions and nuanced terminological distinctions. In my experience as a professor, many students are uncomfortable or unfamiliar with such distinctions. Consequently, they are unwilling to withhold respect from beliefs because they see doing so as a form of intolerance. And so, instead of being a place for vigorous disagreement and debate, the tolerant classroom—and, perhaps, the tolerant society—becomes something else entirely. It is to these tolerant spaces that we now turn, to observe what happens when tolerance is elevated as an unconditional good without clarity about its meaning.

II. When Religious Beliefs Are False (And Some of Them Must Be!)

In pastor Todd Burpo's bestselling book, *Heaven Is for Real*, Burpo recounts his 3-year-old son Colton's recollection of a near-death trip to heaven. Colton describes seeing Jesus's rainbow-colored horse, a sister miscarried by his mother (unknown to him at the time), and his own pint-sized wings, among other details.

As part of a course on theories of religion, I had my students read portions of Colton's account and then asked if he had really gone to heaven. The question got some giggles, but I was surprised when no one took a stand on the truth of his claims. Instead, they remained silent.

"Who am I to say if he's right or wrong?" one young woman finally said. "I mean, if he believes it then it's true for him. Right?"

Professors of religious studies are subject to this bumper-sticker postmodernism on a regular basis. It's true for him so it's true; there's no way to prove beliefs right or wrong; facts are just social constructs—and so on. Head over to the astronomy department or the history department and you won't hear these kinds of comments, at least not nearly as often. No one suggests that just because Holocaust denial exists, the Holocaust might not have happened for people who don't believe in it. When astrophysicist Neil DeGrasse Tyson publicly debunked rapper B.o.B.'s flat-earth theory, people everywhere cheered—and no one suggested that the earth was actually flat for B.o.B. because he believes it—or that Tyson should tolerate the mistaken belief.[14]

But the value of religious tolerance—enshrined in the founding documents of nearly all modern liberal democracies—problematizes the criticism of religious practices and beliefs. When it comes to religion, my students, together with a large portion of the general public, are what Stephen Prothero describes in *God Is Not One* as "good with 'respectful' but allergic to 'argument.'"[15] To tell someone that her identity is bound up with beliefs that are false or pernicious seems to be the very definition of intolerant. Better to *Coexist*, as the popular bumper sticker has it. For this reason, religiously tolerant political systems remain agnostic about religion. Martha Nussbaum puts it well: "Even if governments don't coerce people, the very announcement that a given religion (or antireligion) is the preferred view is a kind of insult to people who in all conscience cannot share this view and wish to continue to go their own way."[16]

Nussbaum allows that although governments should not pronounce on the veracity of religious views, individuals should be able to do so, at least by law. But legislation does not exhaust the reasonable mandates of religious tolerance. As Nussbaum notes, the virtue of civility

14. See, for instance, "Neil deGrasse Tyson fires back at B.o.B with epic mic drop," Lauren Said-Moorhouse, CNN.com, January 29, 2016, http://www.cnn.com/2016/01/29/entertainment/neil-degrasse-tyson-bob-flat-earth-twitter-spat/

15. Stephen Prothero, *God is Not One: The Eight Rival Religions that Rule the World* (New York: HarperOne, 2011), 4.

16. Martha C. Nussbaum, *The New Religious Intolerance: Overcoming the Politics of Fear in an Anxious Age* (Cambridge, Mass.: Harvard University Press, 2012), 241–2.

has extra-legal ramifications for what constitutes intolerance. It may be legal to say to a passing stranger in a hijab that Islam is misogynistic; nevertheless, doing so is uncivil—a clear-cut example, to my mind, of undesirable religious intolerance.

Yet the value of religious tolerance and the associated virtue of civility can tempt people into adopting intellectually irresponsible positions. Clearly it is challenging for many of us to refrain from criticizing other people whose core beliefs we find profoundly misguided or nonsensical—hence the persistent historical need for religious tolerance in the first place. To make tolerance easier, some popular authors and academics preach a comforting vision of religion that renders argument unnecessary, viz., all religions are essentially the same, and therefore fundamentally compatible. Core values are shared; differences are superficial and subjective—an understanding of the world's religions that Prothero diagnoses as widespread and rejects as "dangerous, disrespectful, and untrue." One sees this understanding reflected in comments like those made by Barack Obama on September 10, 2011. "ISIL is not 'Islamic'," he told the American people, no doubt acutely aware of the need to encourage religious tolerance. "No religion condones the killing of innocents."[17] The logic behind his statements is straightforward: If all religions are essentially the same and compatible "with respect to the treatment of innocents," and our own religious convictions count as authentically religious, then ISIL cannot be a religion, for the simple reason that ISIL's stated goals and beliefs are obviously incompatible with a conviction universally held by religions.

But religions—that is, religious doctrines, practices, and believers situated in particular times and places—are not essentially the same, and they are not all compatible. Ancient practices of human sacrifice count as religious, even if we find them repugnant today and would take action to stamp out their revival. Modern-day Catholics may regret the Crusades, but it was a religious act when Pope Urban II start-

17. Office of the Press Secretary, "Statement by the President on ISIL," (Washington, D.C.: The White House, September 10, 2014), https://www.whitehouse.gov/the-press-office/2014/09/10/statement-president-isil-1. The White House prefers the use of "ISIL" (an acronym for "Islamic State in Iraq and the Levant") to "ISIS" (for "Islamic State in Iraq and Syria").

ed them with a cry of *Deus vult!* ("God wills it!") The same is true of contemporary religion. Obama is being intellectually irresponsible when he asserts that ISIL is neither religious nor Islamic. ISIL *is* Islamic and it *is* religious, notwithstanding the existence of pacifist Sufism, which is *also* Islamic and religious.[18]

My students' relativism is a different form of intellectual irresponsibility, though it serves the same purpose: making tolerance easy. Instead of reconciling religions by narrowing the definition of religion, relativism broadens the definition of truth. For those who value civility and religious tolerance, "if it's true for them then it's true" is an easy way out. One can avoid insulting another's religious beliefs by asserting there is no objective way to adjudicate their value or veracity. Better to embrace religious relativism than run the risk of bigotry.[19]

Relativism might work in theory, but it is impossible to implement. Even a government forbidden from elevating one religion over another cannot be consistently relativist. Debates about everything from biology to human rights demonstrate the impossibility of compartmentalizing religious beliefs. Should public education curriculums remain agnostic about the coexistence of humans and dinosaurs, given that it is a matter of religious debate? Should politicians refrain from pronouncing on the inhumanity of religiously inspired violence such as mass shootings and abortion clinic bombings? Surely not, and neither should even the most tolerant of individuals.

The religiously tolerant who refuse relativism (or refuse to pretend to be relativists) have another option, one that many of my students pick: silence. This option makes a great deal of sense in daily life. If one wishes to keep the peace, it is usually best to avoid arguing about

---

18. Elizabeth Hurd suggests that there is a common distinction between two faces of faith, "good religion" and "bad religion." Obama's strategy is to define religion so that it does not include "bad religion." See Hurd, *Beyond Religious Freedom* (Princeton: Princeton University Press, 2015), 22–36.

19. Robert Trigg describes a similar problematic relationship between relativism and tolerance. See his *Religious Diversity* (Cambridge: Cambridge University Press, 2014), 23–27. Rainer Forst argues that it is possible to have "relativization without relativism," but even if it is possible to relativize without relativism, failure seems like a distinct possibility, especially when one is not so philosophically sophisticated as Forst. Rainer Forst, *Toleration in Conflict: Past and Present* (Cambridge: Cambridge University Press, 2013), 22, and also 22 n. 19.

religious beliefs with strangers, and sometimes even with friends and family, say, at a holiday gathering. "In most cases," writes Nussbaum, regarding the controversy over Muslim women's head-coverings, "it's just rude to offer unsolicited opinions about the way a person is dressed, and one risks offense even if one knows the person quite well."[20] I think most people would agree this is wise counsel, particularly if the form of dress in question is religious, as is the case with head-coverings. Indeed, it holds for religious beliefs in general. I am intolerant if I stand in front of a church and inform entering congregants that their worldview is based on childish superstition, even if that is what I really believe.

Of course, no one thinks we must always hold our tongues. Supporters of religious tolerance acknowledge that a certain degree of intolerance is unavoidable, indeed desirable, both in government policies and individual behavior. Some combination of the harm principle (reduce suffering) and respect—in Leiter's sense of *minimal respect*—for universal human rights (respect dignity and autonomy) means that liberal democracies must legislate against certain religious practices that cause suffering to non-consenting agents or otherwise impinge on their human rights. There are also certain beliefs that, while legal to hold, nevertheless deserve public criticism, civility be damned. Nussbaum, for instance, argues that "we all may and should condemn the expression of hatred."[21] It's hard to imagine even the strictest advocates of religious tolerance calling on us to remain silent as Ku Klux Klan members march down our block with burning crosses. *Contra* President Obama, this is an expression, at least in part, of religious convictions, convictions that religiously tolerant people ought not tolerate.

Setting the limits of religious tolerance at harm and hate leaves us in an awkward position when it comes to religious attitudes that are not patently harmful or hateful, but still false and potentially pernicious. It is this position that my students—and I—face when we discuss Colton Burpo's trip to heaven. There's nothing obviously harmful or hateful about believing that the account presented in *Heaven is for*

---

20. Nussbaum, *The New Religious Intolerance*, 118.
21. Ibid.

Real does, in fact, accurately represent reality. Nevertheless, secular and religious commentators have both seen fit to pronounce publicly on its falsehood. In their pronouncements there is a sense of urgency—to believe Burpo isn't merely false, but also betrays some kind of epistemological shortcoming, a failure to consider all the evidence or the inability to weigh it reasonably.

This is a crucial point. Irrational beliefs may be harmless, but irrationality is not. For those who see the trip to heaven as false, it is important to debate the truth of Burpo's account, not because the belief is intrinsically harmful, but rather because *being the type of person who can hold that belief may be harmful.* As Peter Jones writes,

> It might be argued that a genuine state of well-being cannot rest upon beliefs which are evil or erroneous; people cannot really flourish on the basis of unsatisfactory identities. So, if we have an obligation to promote people's well-being and if we confront someone with false beliefs, we must begin by transforming their beliefs and so transforming their identity.[22]

For our purposes here, where Jones says "transforming their beliefs" we can substitute "transforming their belief-forming faculty." False belief is an indication of a faulty belief-forming faculty. It is this faulty belief-forming faculty that endangers people's ability to flourish, and therefore false beliefs must be debated not only because of their potential harmfulness, but also because of the potential harmfulness of a belief-forming faculty that is able to hold them. In the case of those who criticize Burpo's account, intolerance is directed at (potentially harmful) uncritical thinking as much the (potentially harmless) belief that results from it. Like all criticism, it can be civil or rude. But even civil criticism cannot avoid being intolerant and disrespectful, in the sense that it seeks to undermine the belief in question and change the identity of the person who holds it.

If you are seriously invested in religious tolerance, criticizing religious beliefs is difficult because doing so is insulting. It is to tell someone that she has misunderstood the realm of the sacred, and that her misunderstanding is due to a deficiency of knowledge or ability. Yet this is precisely what many people believe about each other's religious beliefs! The vast majority of evangelical Christians regard the Chris-

22. Peter Jones, "Beliefs and Identities," in *Toleration, Identity, and Difference,* ed. by John Horton and Susan Mendus (New York: St. Martin's Press, 1999), 72.

tian Bible as their god's inspired word. Those who do not share their belief are profoundly mistaken—in ways that stand to harm them, and possibly society. Similarly, the so-called New Atheists see all revealed religions as patently false, and attribute belief in them to various intellectual and psychological shortcomings.

To be told that you are incorrect about a deeply held and highly significant belief is (for many) insulting and hurtful, particularly if you already feel underrepresented and persecuted. It feels as if respect for you as a human being—a human whose identity is bound up with religious beliefs—is being violated. Most people can find a good reason to feel underrepresented, even if others disagree with their position. Atheists feel underrepresented: they point to polls that show Americans are less likely to vote for an atheist president than any other demographic. Evangelical Christians feel persecuted: witness the popular trope of the "war on Christmas" and the philosophical complaint that liberalism unfairly squeezes religion out of the "public square" into the private sphere. Muslims in the United States feel underrepresented and persecuted, for reasons that hardly need articulation.

After reflection, then, the religiously tolerant person may judge that we should refrain from any public criticism of religious beliefs, since doing so is insulting and might very reasonably be called hateful and intolerant. This is precisely what happened in late 2015 when the student union at Britain's University of Warwick decided to ban Maryam Namazie, a secular human-rights activist, from speaking on campus. Namazie, an Iranian-born former Muslim, routinely challenges radical Islamist beliefs and criticizes many aspects of Islam. Her positions were found to violate the student union's policy, which forbids external speakers to spread "hatred and intolerance in the community" and says they "must seek to avoid insulting other faiths or groups." Namazie's critical views, the president of the student union concluded, could infringe upon the "right of Muslim students not to feel intimidated or discriminated against on their university campus."[23]

---

23. Serina Sandhu, "Maryam Namazie: Secular activist barred from speaking at Warwick University over fears of 'inciting hatred' against Muslim students," *Independent*, September 25, 2015, http://www.independent.co.uk/news/uk/home-news/maryam-namazie-secular-activist-barred-from-speaking-at-warwick-university-over-fears-of-inciting-10517296.html-0

The student union's decision sparked public outcry, and Namazie was eventually allowed to speak. If the argument I make about the value of religious intolerance holds, then the decision to allow Namazie was a good one. The veracity of religious beliefs, the origins of religious traditions, the purpose and utility of religious practices—these should be the subject of public debate, even if the substance of the debate entails people calling each other damned, ignorant, immoral, or irrational (however euphemistically or circuitously). My students can—and should—feel free to pronounce on the dubiousness or plausibility of Burpo's journey, and they should feel free to defend their religious beliefs or lack thereof without fear of being labeled hateful and close-minded. The alternatives—silence, relativism, or dishonesty about one's beliefs—are unacceptable.

In short: I believe religious intolerance has a valuable and necessary role to play in classrooms and on campuses, the ends of which are crucial to the broader ends of liberal democracy. The rest of this essay defends that claim, first by clarifying the meaning of religious intolerance, and then articulating its place in higher education and, by extension, our shared political and civil culture.

III. The Value of Intolerance

Tolerance has been a central value of liberalism for over three centuries, essential to the peaceful (and desirable) coexistence of people with diverse ideologies, and the foundation for a free "marketplace" of ideas. Yet despite its importance, the definition and proper scope of tolerance remain highly contested. Though he was a foundational figure in the history of religious tolerance, John Locke saw fit to advocate against tolerating Islam and Roman Catholicism. Catholics, he asserted, owed allegiance to no prince but the pope, and therefore could not be trusted to obey a non-Catholic government, and the same was true for Muslims' allegiance to their religious leaders. Nor did Locke sympathize with atheism:

> ...[t]hose are not at all to be tolerated who deny the being of a God. Promises, covenants, and oaths, which are the bonds of human society, can

have no hold upon an atheist. The taking away of God, though but even in thought, dissolves all…[24]

Liberalism is indebted to Locke for articulating enduring liberal justifications of the need for tolerance, but he failed (by all modern criteria) to properly delimit its scope.

The problem of proper scope results in what Rainer Forst calls the "paradox of drawing the limits."[25] The paradox states that "toleration must always flip over into its opposite, intolerance, once it traces the inevitable boundary between what can and cannot be tolerated." This paradox results from attempting to resolve two other paradoxes: the *paradox of self-destruction*, which states that "if toleration extends to the enemies of toleration, it leads to its own destruction," and the *paradox of moral toleration*, which observes that toleration seems to result in the moral rightness of tolerating what is morally wrong or bad. Later, I will argue that collective civil pursuit of truth is a shared moral good. When coupled with the injunction that one should tolerate others' beliefs, this entails a further paradox, the *paradox of epistemological toleration*, which states that it is morally good to tolerate falsehoods believed by others, but also morally good to pursue truth.

Various attempts to resolve these apparent paradoxes proceed by grounding the value of tolerance in other universal norms. Tolerance extends only to those practices and beliefs that do not conflict with basic human rights, say, or Rawlsian ideals of justice and liberalism. The ultimate end of tolerance is not actually toleration, but the realization of specific ideals: human dignity, autonomy, reduced pain, diversity, recognition of the Other, etc. To restrict illiberal beliefs and practices is to be tolerant—or at least not intolerant.

Yet all the attempted resolutions suffer from the same basic flaw, which Stanley Fish states in terms of liberalism (taken to be synonymous with tolerance): "All of liberalism's efforts to accommodate or tame illiberal forces fail, either by underestimating or trivializing the illiberal impulse, or by mirroring it."[26] That is, tolerance either ignores

---

24. John Locke, "A Letter Concerning Toleration" (1697), http://www.constitution.org/jl/tolerati.htm

25. For the paradoxes discussed in this paragraph see Forst, *Toleration in Conflict*, 17–35.

26. Stanley Fish, "Mission Impossible: Settling the Just Bounds Between Church and State," *Columbia Law Review* 97 (8) (1997), 2255–2333. A characteristic autonomy-

the tough cases or refuses to tolerate them. This approach is eminently pragmatic—the only other option is self-destruction. "I do not fault them for [being illiberal]," writes Fish, "but for thinking and claiming to be doing something else."[27] Intolerance by any other name is still intolerance.

Thankfully, diagnosing the problem in this way also points to a potential solution. Fish argues that there is nothing inherently wrong with intolerance or illiberalism—the real issue is with refusing to call a spade a spade. If we accept Fish's willingness to countenance some instances of intolerance, then there is no need to resolve paradoxes with strained definitions of tolerance. Instead, one can simply recognize that intolerance is occasionally valuable and leave it at that.[28] This is the approach I will eventually advocate regarding religious intolerance, *even in the case of religious beliefs that are not obviously hateful or harmful,* such as belief in Colton Burpo's trip to heaven.

Before discussing the potential value of religious intolerance it will be helpful to identify two generally agreed upon characteristics of tolerance:

- *Tolerance requires the presence of beliefs or practices judged false or pernicious.* It is neither indifference nor acceptance.[29] If your friend has different taste in music, it does not make sense to speak of tolerating her taste. This is why embracing religious relativism obviates the need for tolerance; one merely accepts the existence of multiple ways of life, the superiority of which need not (and cannot) be adjudicated. As George Fletcher puts it: "If there is no salvation, or if salvation bears no relation to correct beliefs

---

based response to this sort of objection can be found in Forst, *Toleration in Conflict,* especially chapter 11, "The Virtue of Tolerance." For a response that defends "toleration as recognition," see Anna Elisabetta Galeotti, *Toleration as Recognition* (Cambridge: Cambridge University Press, 2002) esp. chapters 2 and 7.

27. Fish, "Mission Impossible," 2257.

28. This is not a common approach. For some recent examples see John Perry and Nigel Biggar, "Religion and intolerance: A critical commentary," in Steve Clarke, Russell Powell, and Julian Savulescu, eds., *Religion, Intolerance, and Conflict: A Scientific and Conceptual Investigation* (Oxford: Oxford University Press, 2013), 253–265.

29. Forst calls this the "objection component" (Forst 2013, 18). See also Williams 1996, 20, and Cohen 2004, 71.

and practices, I do not see why I should give a hoot whether my neighbor believes in one god or ten."[30]

- *Tolerance can be exercised by multiple types of subjects towards multiple types of objects.* Individuals, communities, and governments can all be tolerant, and they can all be tolerated. I may tolerate my friend's loud praying though it keeps me awake; my community may tolerate prayers blasted over loudspeakers; and a tolerant government may legislate in favor of allowing citizens to blast those prayers, no matter what I or the neighbors want.[31] Similarly, my community's willingness to tolerate prayers blasted over loudspeakers depends on the object of that tolerance: our decision might well be reversed if the number of people blasting those prayers goes from one or two individuals to a sub-community of one hundred or one thousand.

A third commonly stated characteristic of tolerance is that the tolerating subject must have the power to change the beliefs of the object of toleration. For example, consider the definition proposed by the Morrell Centre for Toleration at the University of York:

> …for something to be an instance of toleration, the following features are often thought essential:
> - First, the tolerator must regard the beliefs or practices that are to be tolerated as objectionable (otherwise, the attitude might be closer to "indifference");
> - Second, the tolerator must have the power to interfere to change the beliefs or stop the practices of the tolerated;
> - Third, the tolerator must forbear from such interference (this is sometimes thought to give rise to the "paradox of toleration", if what is claimed is that it is morally virtuous to permit or put up with things that one believes to be morally (or otherwise) "objectionable").[32]

I see significant objections to this position, especially when considered from the perspective of what qualifies as intolerance. There are nu-

---

30. George Fletcher, "The Instability of Tolerance," in *Toleration: An Elusive Virtue*, ed. by David Heyd (Princeton: Princeton University Press, 1996), 160.

31. David Heyd makes a compelling case that "tolerance," strictly speaking, cannot be exercised by governments. Heyd, "Is toleration a political virtue?", in *Toleration and its Limits* (New York: New York University Press, 2008), 171–194.

32. Morrell Center for Toleration, "What is Toleration?," accessed October 16, 2016, https://www.york.ac.uk/morrell-centre-for-toleration/toleration/ , and also Galeotti, *Toleration as Recognition*, 22, n. 6.

merous fringe political groups that have no genuine political power, yet are virulently intolerant. Do they only become intolerant when they shift into a position of genuine political power?

Despite the fact that tolerance can be exercised by multiple types of subjects towards multiple types of objects, it is common practice to consider decontextualized questions of tolerance phrased in the passive voice. However, asking "Should X belief or practice be tolerated?" only makes sense when one is trying to decide whether X identifies an unconditional evil such as slavery, or an unconditional good such as respect for someone's basic human dignity. (The respective answers would be "Never!" and "Always!") The vast majority of beliefs and practices that may or may not qualify for toleration fall between these two poles—if such poles even exist. It is essential, therefore, to contextualize the subject that tolerates and the object of toleration, since doing so determines the answer to the question.

Take, for instance, the belief that the acquisition of personhood through ensoulment does not happen at the moment of conception. Should this belief be tolerated? It depends on the subject and the object of toleration, as well as the context. Understood as the question of whether a liberal democratic government should tolerate the expression of this belief by members of its citizenry, the answer is certainly yes. To state otherwise would be to endorse by proxy public school curriculums that teach the truth of ensoulment and the consequent murderousness of abortion, perhaps even to outlaw the expression of dissent to "life begins at the moment of conception" on the grounds that doing so presented a clear and present danger to the lives of unborn persons. The most basic understanding of religiously tolerant government forbids this kind of religious intolerance.

The answer changes when the object of toleration becomes the government itself. A liberal democratic government should be *intolerant* of official government proclamations against, or for, the truth of ensoulment. Though individual politicians might attempt to issue such a proclamation, other politicians would be justified in acting intolerantly, refusing to grant them permission and attempting to convince them that their beliefs about the proper role of government are mistaken. In this context, with this subject and object, intolerance is now valuable.

But what if the subject is the United States Conference of Catholic Bishops, and the object is belief among American Catholics? It seems perfectly reasonable that the USCCB should teach explicitly, as it does on its website, about the "evil of deliberate killing in abortion." The USCCB should *not* tolerate the belief that abortion is acceptable, or the associated belief that ensoulment does not happen at the moment of conception. If increasing numbers of Catholics question the doctrine of ensoulment, the church should spare no expense putting their questions to rest.

The declaration of abortion as evil is no doubt insulting and offensive to many people, in and outside of the church. It is explicitly intolerant of the belief that abortion should be legal. Nevertheless, it would be absurd to argue that the governing bodies of religious organizations cannot speak publicly about their beliefs with the intent of persuading non-believers. To be the Catholic Church *just is* to be intolerant of falsehoods (*Jesus Christ was just a man*) and to want to replace them with religious truths (*Jesus Christ was both fully human and divine*). Conversely, to be an atheist organization that teaches about the harmful irrationality of religious beliefs *just is* to be intolerant of falsehoods (*Jesus Christ was divine*) and to want to replace them with non-religious truths (*"divine" is a nonsensical category*). In both cases, intolerance is not a shortcoming but rather a natural and necessary aspect of the subject's identity. In both cases the intolerant statements will offend people—indeed, part of their purpose is to change the minds of those who take offense. And in both cases the organizations would maintain—in accordance with their respective foundational beliefs—that religious intolerance is not only a necessary part of their identity but also of value to the general public.

The questions become trickier with individuals, who play more roles than organizations and governments. What if you are a devout Catholic and the potential object of toleration is your neighbors, whose car sports a large *Against Abortion? Don't Have One!* bumper sticker, right next to another that depicts a fish with legs eating an ichthys. Quite reasonably you take these stickers to mean that your neighbors do not believe in ensoulment at conception—or souls at all, for that matter. Should you tolerate their beliefs, or should you intervene and attempt to convince them otherwise? Said differently, should you be intolerant of their beliefs?

On the one hand, you think their beliefs are false and potentially pernicious. Not only that, the bumper stickers themselves are insulting expressions of intolerance for your beliefs. On the other hand, you understand that basic standards of civility require you to mind your own business, and you realize that your own "Jesus is Lord Whether You Believe It Or Not" bumper sticker could also be construed as intolerant. In the end, you refrain from confronting your neighbor directly (tolerance), but you continue to vote for staunchly pro-life political candidates who publicly declare that "life is a gift from god," in hopes they will eventually dominate public discourse and help to convince the general public of your position (intolerance).

As it turns out, your neighbors have made very similar choices. They, too, avoid conversations with you about religion (tolerance), but contribute to a foundation that puts up atheist billboards in hopes that irrational beliefs about "souls" will eventually fade away, and opposition to abortion along with it (intolerance). As a result, you all get along splendidly as neighbors while remaining true to the convictions of your respective consciences, acting intolerantly in the world to stamp out what you understand to be widely held false and pernicious beliefs.

These examples demonstrate the inevitability of religious intolerance, and the extent to which participants in civil discourse ought to understand the appropriate exercise of it as valuable. Opponents and advocates of legalized abortion will usually disagree on whether religiosity should inform one's political position on the matter, and likely disagree on what counts as a "religious" belief in the first place. They will both vote their intolerance and hope the other side loses. And they will both justify the value of this intolerance with the same basic considerations: the intolerance, on balance, results in less overall harm and more human dignity, and avoids violating fundamental human rights. The question is not whether one side is being intolerant, but rather why their considerations of harm and human rights manifest opposing conclusions about how to vote.

Here another set of beliefs comes in. An atheist might tell you that she does not believe in souls. In fact, she sees belief in revealed religion as a force for evil in the world, given that religions are historically violent and misogynistic traditions that mistake superstition and folklore for divinely revealed truths. The abortion issue is a case in point: countless women have suffered—and still suffer—needless harm and violations of their basic human rights because of widespread and mistaken religious beliefs about personhood. A Catholic, on the other hand, might see personhood at conception as a non-negotiable, indeed deeply grounding, truth. Deliberate killing in abortion is "evil," says the USCCB (and Pope Francis), pure and simple. Furthermore, it is unjust and unrealistic to ask religious people to bracket their religious beliefs when considering questions of what ought to count as a person. To protest outside of abortion clinics is intolerant, but far from being harmful or hateful, it is actually a loving attempt to protect basic human rights.[33]

Questions about harm and human rights cannot be settled without reference to the validity and value of religious beliefs, which returns us to Colton Burpo and Maryam Namazie. To pronounce on the validity and value of deeply held religious beliefs is to risk insulting those who disagree with you. It is an act of religious intolerance, the same religiously intolerant act forbidden (in theory) to our government. Like the neighbors who never bring up religion with each other, my students remain silent about Burpo because they do not see the value of religious intolerance. If forced to speak publicly, they are most comfortable taking a relativist position recommended primarily by its inoffensiveness. The student union faced with the prospect of hosting Maryam Namazie also does not see the value of religious intolerance. Best to all get along and avoid voicing beliefs that could be taken as hateful or harmful.

It is a profound mistake, however, to confuse students with neighbors or professors with presidents. Institutions of higher education

---

33. See, for instance, Priestsforlife.org, a website for priests who organize civil disobedience.

are distinctive civic institutions with a shared mission: the production and dissemination of knowledge, and the cultivation of intellectual virtues conducive to the acquisition of true, good beliefs. We—by which I mean the people likely to be reading these words—take the production of knowledge and the cultivation of intellectual virtues to be private and public goods. Individuals benefit from being properly equipped to evaluate claims about the afterlife, or about other religiously grounded claims; and so, in turn, does society. Though we may differ radically in our religious convictions, we can agree that it is beneficial for members of our society to adopt well-informed, intellectually sound positions on religion, the better to decide important questions such as the meaning of life or the legality of abortion. The following section argues that silence and naïve relativism on questions of religion hinder the advancement of this goal, and therefore believers and non-believers should fight to preserve the valuable role of religious intolerance in higher education.

IV. Religious Intolerance and the Ends of Higher Education

In March of 2013, Florida Atlantic University instructor Deandre Poole asked his students to write "Jesus" on a piece of paper and then step on it. One of the students went to a local TV station and reported that he'd been suspended for complaining about the exercise, and it wasn't long before the entire nation knew about Poole and his "Jesus"–stomping religious intolerance.[34]

A heated public debate ensued about the scope and limits of academic freedom. The debate was generally framed as a conflict between educators' freedom to challenge deeply held beliefs and their duty to be religiously tolerant. Poole reported that his student accosted him after class, repeatedly asking, "How dare you disrespect someone's religion?" In a letter to the chancellor of FAU, Florida Governor Rick Scott also accused Poole of intolerance: "The professor's lesson was

---

34. For coverage of the incident and an interview with Poole, see Scott Jaschik, "I was just doing my job," *Inside Higher Ed,* April 1, 2013, https://www.insidehighered.com/news/2013/04/01/interview-professor-center-jesus-debate-florida-atlantic

offensive, and even intolerant, to Christians and those of all faiths who deserve to be respected as Americans entitled to religious freedom."[35] To give the exercise was, in other words, an unacceptable exercise of religious intolerance on Poole's part that failed to adequately respect at least one student's religious beliefs.

But what, exactly, was unacceptable about Poole's exercise—and what definition of religious tolerance does that accusation imply? Stanley Fish answers this question by asserting that religious tolerance in the university requires giving students a space where they can consider questions intellectually without having to put their own identities on the line. Educators cross a line, argued Fish in the *New York Times*, when they force students "to *do* something that brings to the surface, out in the open, some of their deepest commitments."[36] In Poole's class, the student was "put in a position where a confrontation with his innermost being could not be avoided; no room to hide." For Fish, the exercise would have been acceptable had Poole restricted his instruction to "think about what you'd do" instead of "do this." The problem is that Poole requires students "to get out of their chairs and *do* something." Civil debate about religion is fine, provided that it does not force students to act.

But Fish's distinction between thinking and doing breaks down if we use it to describe a classroom discussion of religion. The first problem is that thinking and doing cannot be distinguished as though the former occurs without the latter. In reality, thinking, especially in higher education, often involves all kinds of doing. Professors ask students to raise their hands, to move their mouths, to type papers and hand them in, to sit in class and take exams, to ask and answer questions. (What are chemistry students in a lab doing? Just thinking?) True, Poole could have made his exercise a thought experiment, as Fish suggests he should have. But the ensuing vigorous discussion that Fish imagines would not subsequently be restricted to "acts of the mind," unless talking and looking and gesturing and saying "I be-

---

35. Scott's letter is available online through the *Miami Herald*: http://miamiherald.typepad.com/files/scott-letter-about-fau-incident.pdf.

36. Stanley Fish, "Stepping on Jesus," *New York Times*, April 15, 2013 (emphasis added), http://opinionator.blogs.nytimes.com/2013/04/15/stepping-on-jesus

lieve Christianity is false" aren't really "overt acts." As we have seen, in the classroom the only way to prevent beliefs about what is true from turning into actions is by remaining silent.[37]

When it comes to religion, what Fish characterizes as "acts of the mind" or "contemplation" can also confront you with your innermost being; it can leave you with no room to hide. In my *Religions of the World* course many students are shaken when they learn that Jesus never explicitly mentions homosexuals, or that there are in fact two biblical creation stories. My Muslim hijab-wearing students are no doubt personally affected by reading assigned opinion pieces on the oppressiveness of head scarves. Atheist students who think religion is just superstition may reconsider their position after meeting kind, intelligent, articulate defenders of religious faith.

Even if we accept that the thinking/doing division disallows Poole's exercise, it's hard to conceive of a rigorous academic discussion of religious epistemology—What is the authority of the Christian Bible? How does one interpret it properly?—that does not admit for sincere consideration beliefs that some people might find insulting or deeply troubling. Pretending that the "mere" contemplation of ideas cannot be existentially significant makes it difficult to understand the historical popularity of censorship.

In itself, none of this serves to validate the "Jesus"-stepping activity. It may be that Poole was excessively confrontational, or failed to explain sufficiently the significance of the exercise, or made any number of mistakes that can result in a lousy learning experience. Important questions remain about the limits of academic discourse. (Can a professor ask students to engage in a vivid thought experiment in which Jesus is a human deceiver who pulled off a hoax? Did I ask you to do so simply by writing those words? Is reading an "act" of the mind?) What should be clear, however, is that requiring students and faculty to confront, question, and defend their innermost being and deepest commitments is not unacademic. Poole's activity might have been

---

37. In a 1943 decision, the Supreme Court recognized the overlap of beliefs, statements of belief, and actions when it ruled that "the flag salute is a form of utterance," and compelling a student to salute was coercive—"to compel him to utter what is not in his mind." *West Virginia State Board of Education v. Barnette*, 319 U.S. 624 (1943), 634. See Appendix, infra, 45.

wrong, but not, as Governor Scott suggests, because it was intolerant, nor, as Fish suggests, because it forced students to confront their innermost being. Neither of these are, in themselves, impermissible in universities.

No doubt there are some educators uncomfortable with Poole's approach to pedagogy, especially in the religious studies classroom. Introductory courses on religion can be—and often are—taught as surveys of beliefs and behaviors, bracketing discussion of the historical or philosophical validity of a particular tradition's claims. But teaching religion in this way isolates it from every other discipline. Teachers of history or biology do not simply survey beliefs about the identity of the early inhabitants of the Americas, or the various beliefs that people have had about evolution. Philosophers do not simply survey the various ethical positions held by different people at different times. To do good history, or biology, or philosophy, is to recognize not only that people have held a variety of beliefs for a variety of reasons, but also that certain of these beliefs are false and therefore not worth holding. The disinterested search for truth, one of the secular academy's central ideals, necessitated the expulsion of fideism and apologist curricula from classrooms. But claiming that no religion has a monopoly on truth is not the same as claiming that no religion is wrong. The disinterested search for truth also means that one cannot bracket off a particular kind of belief as immune from criticism, especially when those beliefs overlap with other disciplines. This is the paradox of epistemological toleration—to pursue truth as morally good is incompatible with tolerating belief in falsehoods, no matter how important those falsehoods are to someone's identity.

Indeed, the essential purpose and unique objective of higher education requires a space where religiously intolerant confrontations can take place, confrontations that force the sort of existential challenges that unnerve Fish. Needless to say, this is not the end of public parks or sidewalks, which would be miserable failures if using them involved actively justifying your religious convictions in response to the criticisms of passing citizens. The academy is different. To produce knowledge and cultivate intellectual virtues we must challenge ourselves through lived encounters with different ways of being in the world. Edward Said uses the metaphor of academia as existential travel, unifying thought and action in the lived life:

> The image of traveler depends not on power, but on motion, on a willingness to go into different worlds, use different idioms, and understand a variety of disguises, masks, and rhetorics. Travelers must suspend the claim of customary routine in order to live in new rhythms and rituals.[38]

With regard to Poole, it could be argued that students were being *coerced* into traveling, and it is for that reason their journey failed. The pursuit of truth requires open and willing dialogue, which is incompatible with coercion. Perhaps before being forced to take a journey, especially a journey that calls their own sense of self into question, students need to understand why traveling is important—that is, the goal of the pedagogue should be to explain the virtue of disinterested academic inquiry, here instantiated as the performative act of stepping on a piece of paper inscribed with "Jesus," before forcing students into it. But this does not negate the main thrust of the argument, which is that religious intolerance is not a bad thing. Students and teachers, like anyone interested in truth, must ask themselves what will encourage others to adopt true beliefs. In some cases silence will be best, or a gentle introduction to the principles of disinterested inquiry. The problem with Poole's exercise is not its intolerance, but rather its ineffectiveness.

Eliminating spaces dedicated to secular academic inquiry impedes the production of knowledge, and for this reason academic free speech is of singular importance in liberal democracy. "Academic freedom is not just a nice job perk," writes Louis Menand. "It is the philosophical key to the whole enterprise of higher education," which, stated plainly, is "simply the production and dissemination of knowledge—that is, research and teaching."[39] The enterprise of producing and disseminating knowledge is a "democratic ideal," and so higher education is a civic good.[40] Menand's position recalls Justice Brennan's majority opinion in *Keyishian vs. the Board of Regents*, which declared uncon-

---

38. Edward Said, *Reflections on Exile and Other Essays* (Cambridge, Mass.: Harvard University Press, 2000), 404.

39. Louis Menand, *The Marketplace of Ideas: Reform and Resistance in the American University* (New York: W. W. Norton, 2010), 131.

40. Id. at 13.

stitutional the firing of instructors who refused to sign documents stating they were not Communists, as required under New York's teacher loyalty laws. "Our Nation is deeply committed to safeguarding academic freedom," opined Brennan, "which is of transcendent value to all of us and not merely to the teachers concerned. That freedom is therefore a special concern of the First Amendment, which does not tolerate laws that cast a pall of orthodoxy over the classroom."[41]

The history of intellectual progress is humbling and instructive. Time and time again, controversial views transform from heresies into accepted scientific and moral truths, whether the theory of evolution or the equal dignity of races. A certain degree of orthodoxy on religious matters is clearly necessary in churches, and non-confrontational religious tolerance—an orthodoxy of silence—should probably govern our interactions in the supermarket. But designated spaces for the unfettered investigation of unorthodox perspectives must be preserved for the sake of our collective civil investment in truth. That some of these perspectives may be insulting, offensive, treasonous, or blasphemous cannot disqualify them from consideration.

Nor can we forget about the cultivation of intellectual virtues, which is related to but distinct from the production and dissemination of knowledge. Students and faculty alike also need academic freedom to become the kind of people who are more likely to adopt and act upon true beliefs. As Justice Brennan recognizes in *Keyishian*, curtailing freedom of expression and association has a "stifling effect on the academic mind."[42] Pressure to be religiously tolerant curtails academic freedom of expression because straightforward statements about one's religious convictions—"only Christians are saved"; "people who oppose homosexual marriage are cruel"—are quite reasonably understood to be intolerant, insulting, disrespectful, and therefore taboo. The result of this pressure is classrooms and campuses where students can expect to be educated without having to articulate and defend their deepest religious commitments (or lack thereof). In seeking to become a place of "unconstrained agreements," argues Alasdair

---

41. *Keyishian, et al. v. Board of Regents of the University of the State of New York, et al.*, 385 U.S. 589 (1967), 603. Appendix, infra, 62.

42. Id. at 607.

MacIntyre, liberal education has had to purge itself of "fundamental debate on moral and theological questions."[43]

This religiously sanitized version of higher education makes it difficult to develop intellectual virtues such as consistency, integrity, and courage—virtues of what Brennan calls the academic mind. We are all intellectually deficient, susceptible to bias, fear, and complacency. Perhaps our worst failing is intellectual inconsistency, which helps us maintain self-serving views. "Criticizing others for something you are also guilty of—what a ubiquitous human failing," as Nussbaum observes.[44] Her solution is for us to courageously examine our beliefs and have the integrity to recognize when we are being inconsistent. We must listen generously and seek, in dialogue, our own inevitable mistakes and blind spots. When beliefs we do not accept are part of someone's religious worldview, we do not make snap judgments about the quality of the person who holds those beliefs.

Without intolerance, however, the process falls apart. Academic dialogue about religion requires us to speak our minds about religious truths, even if others find our perspective insulting. To whom are we listening generously and openly, if not someone who possesses the courage and integrity to tell us we are wrong? How can we cultivate the intellectual virtues of epistemic humility and fallibilism if no one points out our errors and challenges our convictions? Religious intolerance, that is, withholding respect from certain religious beliefs, being clear about your reasons for doing so, and seeking the disappearance of the beliefs you do not respect, is a necessary ingredient in authentic interreligious dialogue, for the same reason that general pursuit of knowledge depends on regular old intolerance of falsehood. Whereas civility on the street requires people to avoid intellectual conflict, civility in the classroom does not. There, it is a virtue to speak your mind honestly and listen to others speak theirs, even when what gets said threatens people's most deeply held religious commitments. Truth, as they say, can hurt, but it will also set you free.

---

43. Alasdair MacIntyre, *Three Rival Versions of Moral Enquiry* (Notre Dame: University of Notre Dame Press, 1990), 230, 221.

44. Nussbaum, *The New Religious Intolerance*, 100.

Some may fear that religious intolerance could work against the possibility of interfaith dialogue in higher education. In fact, the opposite is true. Intellectually honest people, religious or not, care deeply about truth. They want to make sure their own beliefs are worth holding and they think others are better off doing the same. Interfaith dialogue is an opportunity not only to learn about other people's beliefs, but also to challenge the basis of those beliefs and allow them to challenge one's own. As former vice provost of Duke University Robert Thompson puts it: "Having to clarify, critically analyze, and defend one's religious and moral positions—just as one would do with claims about science, economics, or political theory—is part of the learning experience and identity formation process."[45]

When, for the sake of tolerance, religious truths are homogenized or diminished to a matter of perspective, interfaith dialogue becomes a middle-school art show, where everyone *oohs* and *ahhs* and praises the work without passing judgment on its quality, lest they hurt someone's feelings. This version of dialogue cheapens convictions about religion by reducing them to taste, and disrespects the participants by treating them like children. The opportunity for critical analysis and clarification is lost, just as it is if we avoid the dialogue entirely.

Meanwhile religious intolerance will live on, as it must by necessity, in other arenas. People will continue to vote one way or another on abortion and homosexual marriage and the rights of Muslim immigrants. They will attend churches that preach the exclusive revealed truth of one religion; they will talk with like-minded friends about the irrationality of religion; they will bemoan religious judgmentalism of every variety and purchase *Coexist* bumper-stickers—people will do all these things, but without the benefit of genuine interreligious dialogue, fewer of them will have critically analyzed the beliefs that animate their actions or defended them to someone who disagrees.

Modern liberal education is supposed to combine the Socratic ideal of the examined life with a Millian marketplace of ideas. The product, ideally, is individuals who have cultivated intellectual virtues and ideas that have emerged victorious from communal debate. The communal

---

45. Robert J. Thompson, *Beyond Reason and Tolerance: The Purpose and Practice of Higher Education* (New York: Oxford University Press, 2014), 117.

aspect of the debate is important. It demands patience, open-mindedness, empathy, the courage to question oneself and attempt to see things as others do, a humbled recognition of the fact that we are all in this quest for knowledge together. But real academic debate, though it takes place in a community, is also combat. The ideal liberal university is a place of "constrained disagreement," writes MacIntyre, "of imposed participation in conflict, in which a central responsibility of higher education would be to initiate students into conflict."[46]

In this ideal university we are free to challenge each other on anything, to examine other people's lives in addition to our own, to disrespect entire religious traditions by judging them false. We can engage in MacIntyre's "antagonistic dialogue between fundamentally conflicting and incommensurable standpoints which moral and theological enquiry may be held to require."[47] We can be religiously intolerant. We must be, or there is no real conflict, no antagonistic dialogue, no competitive marketplace, no confrontation with your innermost being or the innermost being of others. Impious, disrespectful, intolerant Socrates disappears as he did in Athens, executed for the crime of refusing to tolerate people's most deeply held beliefs. We are left with Fish's academy rather than Poole's, a safe place where, to use Fish's words from his column, there is a moratorium on students and faculty bringing "to the surface, out in the open, some of their deepest commitments and anxieties," where having room to hide takes precedence over being challenged to change.[48] This loss of a civic space set aside for constrained combat between fundamentally conflicting moral and religious convictions would be a tragedy.

Just as there is a difference between campuses and grocery stores, there is also a difference between different spaces on campus. Students and teachers expect different norms to govern offices, dorm rooms, and classrooms. These can be thought of as forming an arc: at one end are spaces in which people expect not to be engaged in dialogues about their religious beliefs—the bathroom, say, or one's personal residence. At the other end are spaces explicitly dedicated to the pursuit of truth.

46. MacIntyre, *Three Rival Versions of Moral Enquiry*, 231.

47. Id. at 221.

48. Fish, "Stepping on Jesus."

This arc corresponds to a hierarchy of values. Do not knock on people's dorm room doors and tell them they are going to hell, because that is not what one does in dorms. Do not stand on the table in the cafeteria and read aloud from Richard Dawkins's *The God Delusion*. Intolerance meets civility in a spaces meant for privacy, and results in silence. But feel free to tell people that their beliefs relegate them to damnation in the context of a religious studies classroom—intolerance meets civility in a space meant for pursuing truth, and results in debate.

Allowing religious intolerance does not mean everything goes. Intellectual disagreements, as MacIntyre points out, are constrained. American football can be punishingly brutal, but it is still a rule-governed affair. (Without the violence football becomes flag-football, a very different sport with very different ends.) Like all rational discourse, the discourse of higher education depends on what Jurgen Habermas calls "the fundamental norms of rational speech."[49] I have never encountered a better enumeration of the basics than this one by economist and philosopher Deirdre McCloskey: "Don't lie; pay attention; don't sneer; cooperate; don't shout; don't resort to violence or conspiracy in aid of your ideas."[50] To these we may also add that not every moment or space is appropriate for a debate: don't force arguments where they don't belong. That, not intolerance, is uncivil, disrespectful, and ineffective, and therefore inadvisable.

There can be no real dialogue without such principles; they have normative force because of their practical necessity. But as Richard Rorty emphasizes, simply listing abstract rules of undistorted rational conversation is not enough—just as it is not enough to say that religious intolerance belongs in higher education. What counts as a sneer or as shouting can vary dramatically from one culture to the next, and so, too, will definitions of religion. "The pragmatist [...] must remain ethnocentric and offer examples," cautions Rorty.[51]

---

49. Jürgen Habermas (tr. Jeremy J. Shapiro), *Knowledge and Human Interests* (Boston: Beacon Press, 1971), 310.

50. Deirdre McCloskey, *The Rhetoric of Economics* (Madison, Wisc.: University of Wisconsin Press, 1985), 24.

51. Richard Rorty, "Pragmatism, Relativism, and Irrationalism," in *Consequences of Pragmatism* (Minneapolis: University of Minnesota Press, 1982), 173.

Very well: I will offer examples. It is these norms, I believe, that rule out chanting "You killed Jesus" at a basketball game—as Catholic Memorial high school students did when playing against Newton South, a public high school with a large Jewish population. Basketball games are not spaces for theological debate. Catholic Memorial fans were not even interested in a debate; they weren't paying attention; they were shouting.[52] The same rules apply in the example I gave above, of the person who tells a passing stranger in a hijab that Islam is misogynistic. The supermarket and the public sidewalk are reserved for the ordinary activities of everyday life.

Setting apart the academy as a special place may be cause for concern among those who see an anti-intellectual backlash in society, particularly the world of politics. In response, it should be pointed out that the anti-intellectualism, if one wishes to call it that, often marches hand in hand with accusations of political correctness. Allowing for the open expression of one's beliefs about religious truths, whether the exclusive truth of one's own faith or the falseness of others, helps to mitigate the image of higher education as a place where censorship reigns and sensitivity dictates a kind of forced cultural relativism. (In this sense, perhaps part of what appears as anti-intellectualism is actually a valid criticism of problems in higher education.)

Needless to say, there will be hard cases—the case of Harper handing out pamphlets on campus, or students protesting the existence of Israel. Yet these cases are hard not because the activities involved are intolerant, but rather because they challenge dialogical norms and norms of civility. And however such cases get decided, we must make our decisions without sacralizing tolerance and respect. Higher education provides a civic space where believing in falsehoods and making bad arguments are graver sins than disrespect or intolerance—indeed, a space where certain kinds of disrespect and intolerance are virtues, not sins.

---

52. Valerie Strauss, "Fans cheering for Catholic high school basketball team shout 'You killed Jesus' to opposing players," *Washington Post*, March 12, 2016, https://www.washingtonpost.com/news/answer-sheet/wp/2016/03/12/fans-cheering-for-catholic-basketball-team-shout-you-killed-jesus-to-opposing-players/

If we refuse to sacralize tolerance, the twin orthodoxies of silence and relativism will wither. As a result, we will preserve spaces where people can develop the intellectual virtues of humility and fallibilism alongside intellectual courage and love of truth. Students and faculty alike will develop the ability to discuss religion openly and honestly—a civic virtue that is badly needed in the public sphere. And though I cannot know what the results of those discussions will be—which beliefs will be abandoned and which embraced—I have no doubt that our collective journey towards truth and goodness benefits if it is informed, at least in part, by religious intolerance.

Appendix:
Majority opinions in two cases

Reprinted in this appendix are the majority opinions in two Supreme Court cases that feature prominently in the essay above. *West Virginia Board of Education v. Barnette*, typically shortened to *Barnette*, concerns the rights of the children of a religious minority—in this case, Jehovah's Witnesses—to refuse to participate in the recitation of the Pledge of Allegiance, on the grounds that doing so placed them in the position of violating their understanding of the Bible (specifically the Second Commandment). *Keyishian, et al., v. Regents of the University of the State of New York, et al.*, generally shortened to *Keyishian*, concerns academic freedom on the campus of a publicly supported institution of higher education—in this case, freedom to ascribe to a set of ideas generally regarded as Communist, or to associate with like-minded people.

In reprinting these opinions, we have left intact the idiosyncratic way in which Supreme Court opinions do the work of citing their sources. So, for example, an opinion of the court itself is often cited with a style like "319 U.S. 624"—the citation for *Barnette*—which translates to "volume 319 of *United States Reports*, beginning at page 624"; and "*Dombrowski v. Pfister*, 380 U.S. 479, 489-490" means that the opinion is quoting material from a previous decision in the case of *Dombrowski v. Pfister*, at a specific place (pages 489 and 490) within that case (which begins at page 479 of volume 380 of *United States Reports*).

United States Reports is the official record of the Supreme Court; and in rendering its opinions, the Supreme Court often cites previous opinions of its own (indeed, *Keyishian* cites *Barnette*) and of lower federal courts. These are found in a variety of sources, including the *Federal Reporter*, first, second, and third series (denoted F., F.2d., and F.3d.), containing the records of federal district and appellate court proceedings; the decisions of state appellate courts, gathered in a series of volumes gathering opinions in geographic areas, for example the *North Eastern Reporter*, first and second series (N.E. and N.E. 2d); and so on. Readers will also note that the ways in which a Supreme Court opinion cites materials other than court opinions varies somewhat from the usual style of footnotes; we have left this intact here.

The reader will notice the appearance of numbers within brackets (like this: [603]). These indicate the pagination of the original text of the opinion as found in *United States Reports*.

SUPREME COURT OF THE UNITED STATES

WEST VIRIGINIA BOARD OF EDUCATION V. BARNETTE
(319 U.S. 624)

Argued: March 11, 1943

Decided: June 14, 1943

MR. JUSTICE JACKSON delivered the opinion of the Court.
Following the decision by this Court on June 3, 1940, in *Minersville School District v. Gobitis*, 310 U.S. 586, the West Virginia legislature amended its statutes to require all schools therein to conduct courses of instruction in history, civics, and in the Constitutions of the United States and of the State for the purpose of teaching, fostering and perpetuating the ideals, principles and spirit of Americanism, and increasing the knowledge of the organization and machinery of the government.

Appellant [626] Board of Education was directed, with advice of the State Superintendent of Schools, to "prescribe the courses of study covering these subjects" for public schools. The Act made it the duty of private, parochial and denominational schools to prescribe courses of study "similar to those required for the public schools."[1]

---

1. §134, West Virginia Code (1941 Supp.):

In all public, private, parochial and denominational schools located within this state there shall be given regular courses of instruction in history of the United States, in civics, and in the constitutions of the United States and of the State of West Virginia, for the purpose of teaching, fostering and perpetuating the ideals, principles and spirit of Americanism, and increasing the knowledge of the organization and machinery of the government of the United States and of the state of West Virginia. The state board of education shall, with the advice of the state superintendent of schools,

The Board of Education on January 9, 1942, adopted a resolution containing recitals taken largely from the Court's *Gobitis* opinion and ordering that the salute to the flag become "a regular part of the program of activities in the public schools," that all teachers and pupils shall be required to participate in the salute honoring the Nation represented by the Flag; provided, however, that refusal to salute the Flag be regarded as an act of insubordination, and shall be dealt with accordingly.[2]

---

prescribe the courses of study covering these subjects for the public elementary and grammar schools, public high schools and state normal schools. It shall be the duty of the officials or boards having authority over the respective private, parochial and denominational schools to prescribe courses of study for the schools under their control and supervision similar to those required for the public schools.

2. The text is as follows:

WHEREAS, The West Virginia State Board of Education holds in highest regard those rights and privileges guaranteed by the Bill of Rights in the Constitution of the United States of America and in the Constitution of West Virginia, specifically, the first amendment to the Constitution of the United States as restated in the fourteenth amendment to the same document and in the guarantee of religious freedom in Article III of the Constitution of this State, and

WHEREAS, The West Virginia State Board of Education honors the broad principle that one's convictions about the ultimate mystery of the universe and man's relation to it is placed beyond the reach of law; that the propagation of belief is protected, whether in church or chapel, mosque or synagogue, tabernacle or meeting house; that the Constitutions of the United States and of the State of West Virginia assure generous immunity to the individual from imposition of penalty for offending, in the course of his own religious activities, the religious views of others, be they a minority or those who are dominant in the government, but

WHEREAS, The West Virginia State Board of Education recognizes that the manifold character of man's relations may bring his conception of religious duty into conflict with the secular interests of his fellow man; that conscientious scruples have not, in the course of the long struggle for religious toleration, relieved the individual from obedience to the general law not aimed at the promotion or restriction of the religious beliefs; that the mere possession of convictions which contradict the relevant concerns of political society does not relieve the citizen from the discharge of political responsibility, and

WHEREAS, The West Virginia State Board of Education holds that national unity is the basis of national security; that the flag of our Nation is the symbol of our National Unity transcending all internal differences, however large, within the framework of the Constitution; that the Flag is the symbol of the Nation's power; that emblem of freedom in its truest, best sense; that it signifies government resting on the consent of the governed, liberty regulated by law, protection of the weak against the strong, security against the exercise of arbitrary power, and absolute safety for free institutions against foreign aggression, and

WHEREAS, The West Virginia State Board of Education maintains that the public schools, established by the legislature of the State of West Virginia under the

[627]The resolution originally required the "commonly accepted salute to the Flag," which it defined. Objections to the salute as "being too much like Hitler's" were raised by the Parent and Teachers Association, the Boy and Girl [628] Scouts, the Red Cross, and the Federation of Women's Clubs.[3] Some modification appears to have been made in deference to these objections, but no concession was made to Jehovah's Witnesses.[4] What is now required is the "stiff-arm" salute, the saluter to keep the right hand raised with palm turned up while the following is repeated:

> I pledge allegiance to the Flag of the United States of [629] America and to the Republic for which it stands; one Nation, indivisible, with liberty and justice for all.

Failure to conform is "insubordination," dealt with by expulsion. Readmission is denied by statute until compliance. Meanwhile, the ex-

---

authority of the Constitution of the State of West Virginia and supported by taxes imposed by legally constituted measures, are dealing with the formative period in the development in citizenship that the Flag is an allowable portion of the program of schools thus publicly supported.

Therefore, be it RESOLVED, That the West Virginia Board of Education does hereby recognize and order that the commonly accepted salute to the Flag of the United States — the right hand is placed upon the breast, and the following pledge repeated in unison: "I pledge allegiance to the Flag of the United States of America and to the Republic for which it stands; one Nation, indivisible, with liberty and justice for all" -- now becomes a regular part of the program of activities in the public schools, supported in whole or in part by public funds, and that all teachers as defined by law in West Virginia and pupils in such schools shall be required to participate in the salute, honoring the Nation represented by the Flag; provided, however, that refusal to salute the Flag be regarded as an act of insubordination, and shall be dealt with accordingly.

3. The National Headquarters of the United States Flag Association takes the position that the extension of the right arm in this salute to the flag is not the Nazi-Fascist salute, although quite similar to it. In the Pledge to the Flag, the right arm is extended and raised, palm UPWARD, whereas the Nazis extend the arm practically *straight to the front* (the finger tips being about even with the eyes), *palm DOWNWARD*, and the Fascists do the same, except they raise the arm slightly higher.

James A. Moss, *The Flag of the United States: Its History and Symbolism* (1914), 108.

4. They have offered, in lieu of participating in the flag salute ceremony "periodically and publicly," to give the following pledge:

> I have pledged my unqualified allegiance and devotion to Jehovah, the Almighty God, and to His Kingdom, for which Jesus commands all Christians to pray.

> I respect the flag of the United States, and acknowledge it as a symbol of freedom and justice to all.

> I pledge allegiance and obedience to all the laws of the United States that are consistent with God's law, as set forth in the Bible.

pelled child is "unlawfully absent,"5 and may be proceeded against as a delinquent.6 His parents or guardians are liable to prosecution,7 and, if convicted, are subject to fine not exceeding $50 and Jail term not exceeding thirty days.8

Appellees, citizens of the United States and of West Virginia, brought suit in the United States District Court for themselves and others similarly situated asking its injunction to restrain enforcement of these laws and regulations against Jehovah's Witnesses. The Witnesses are an unincorporated body teaching that the obligation imposed by law of God is superior to that of laws enacted by temporal government. Their religious beliefs include a literal version of Exodus, Chapter 20, verses 4 and 5, which says:

> Thou shalt not make unto thee any graven image, or any likeness of anything that is in heaven above, or that is in the earth beneath, or that is in the water under the earth; thou shalt not bow down thyself to them nor serve them.

They consider that the flag is an "image" within this command. For this reason, they refuse to salute it.[630]

Children of this faith have been expelled from school and are threatened with exclusion for no other cause. Officials threaten to send them to reformatories maintained for criminally inclined juveniles. Parents of such children have been prosecuted, and are threatened with prosecutions for causing delinquency.

The Board of Education moved to dismiss the complaint, setting forth these facts and alleging that the law and regulations are an unconstitutional denial of religious freedom, and of freedom of speech, and are invalid under the "due process" and "equal protection" clauses

---

5. § 1851(1), West Virginia Code (1941 Supp.):

If a child be dismissed, suspended, or expelled from school because of refusal of such child to meet the legal and lawful requirements of the school and the established regulations of the county and/or state board of education, further admission of the child to school shall be refused until such requirements and regulations be complied with. Any such child shall be treated as being unlawfully absent from school during the time he refuses to comply with such requirements and regulations, and any person having legal or actual control of such child shall be liable to prosecution under the provisions of this article for the absence of such child from school.

6. § 4904(4), West Virginia Code (1941 Supp.).

7. *See* Note 5, *supra.*

8. §§ 1847, 1851, West Virginia Code (1941 Supp.).

of the Fourteenth Amendment to the Federal Constitution. The cause was submitted on the pleadings to a District Court of three judges. It restrained enforcement as to the plaintiffs and those of that class. The Board of Education brought the case here by direct appeal.[9]

This case calls upon us to reconsider a precedent decision, as the Court, throughout its history, often has been required to do.[10] Before turning to the *Gobitis* case, however, it is desirable to notice certain characteristics by which this controversy is distinguished.

The freedom asserted by these appellees does not bring them into collision with rights asserted by any other individual. It is such conflicts which most frequently require intervention of the State to determine where the rights of one end and those of another begin. But the refusal of these persons to participate in the ceremony does not interfere with or deny rights of others to do so. Nor is there any question in this case that their behavior is peaceable and orderly. The sole conflict is between authority and rights of the individual. The State asserts power to condition access to public education on making a prescribed sign and profession and at the same time to coerce [631] attendance by punishing both parent and child. The latter stand on a right of self-determination in matters that touch individual opinion and personal attitude.

As the present CHIEF JUSTICE said in dissent in the *Gobitis* case, the State may

> require teaching by instruction and study of all in our history and in the structure and organization of our government, including the guaranties of civil liberty, which tend to inspire patriotism and love of country.

310 U.S. at 604. Here, however, we are dealing with a compulsion of students to declare a belief. They are not merely made acquainted with the flag salute so that they may be informed as to what it is or even what it means. The issue here is whether this slow and easily neglected[11] route to aroused loyalties constitutionally may be short-cut by

---

9. § 266 of the Judicial Code, 28 U.S.C. § 380.

10.. *See* authorities cited in *Helvering v. Griffiths*, 318 U.S. 371, 401, note 52.

11. *See* the nationwide survey of the study of American history conducted by the *New York Times*, the results of which are published in the issue of June 21, 1942, and are there summarized on p. 1, col. 1, as follows:

substituting a compulsory salute and slogan.[12] This issue is not prejudiced by [632] the Court's previous holding that, where a State, without compelling attendance, extends college facilities to pupils who voluntarily enroll, it may prescribe military training as part of the course without offense to the Constitution. It was held that those who take advantage of its opportunities may not, on ground of conscience, refuse compliance with such conditions. *Hamilton v. Regents*, 293 U.S. 245. In the present case, attendance is not optional. That case is also to be distinguished from the present one, because, independently of college privileges or requirements, the State has power to raise militia and impose the duties of service therein upon its citizens.

There is no doubt that, in connection with the pledges, the flag salute is a form of utterance. Symbolism is a primitive but effective way of communicating ideas. The use of an emblem or flag to symbolize some system, idea, institution, or personality is a short-cut from mind to mind. Causes and nations, political parties, lodges, and ecclesiastical groups seek to knit the loyalty of their followings to a flag or banner, a color or design. The State announces rank, function, and authority through crowns and maces, uniforms and black robes; the church speaks through the Cross, the Crucifix, the altar and shrine,

---

82 percent of the institutions of higher learning in the United States do not require the study of United States history for the undergraduate degree. Eighteen percent of the colleges and universities require such history courses before a degree is awarded. It was found that many students complete their four years in college without taking any history courses dealing with this country.

Seventy-two percent of the colleges and universities do not require United States history for admission, while 28 percent require it. As a result, the survey revealed, many students go through high school, college and then to the professional or graduate institution without having explored courses in the history of their country.

Less than 10 percent of the total undergraduate body was enrolled in United States history classes during the Spring semester just ended. Only 8 percent of the freshman class took courses in United States history, although 30 percent was enrolled in European or world history courses.

12. The Resolution of the Board of Education did not adopt the flag salute because it was claimed to have educational value. It seems to have been concerned with promotion of national unity (*see* footnote 2), which justification is considered later in this opinion. No information as to its educational aspect is called to our attention except Olander, Children's Knowledge of the Flag Salute, 35 Journal of Educational Research 300, 305, which sets forth a study of the ability of a large and representative number of children to remember and state the meaning of the flag salute which they recited each day in school. His conclusion was that it revealed "a rather pathetic picture of our attempts to teach children not only the words, but the meaning, of our Flag Salute."

and clerical raiment. Symbols of State often convey political ideas, just as religious symbols come to convey theological ones. Associated with many of these symbols are appropriate gestures of acceptance or respect: a salute, a bowed or bared head, a bended knee. A person gets from a [633] symbol the meaning he puts into it, and what is one man's comfort and inspiration is another's jest and scorn.

Over a decade ago, Chief Justice Hughes led this Court in holding that the display of a red flag as a symbol of opposition by peaceful and legal means to organized government was protected by the free speech guaranties of the Constitution. *Stromberg v. California*, 283 U.S. 359. Here, it is the State that employs a flag as a symbol of adherence to government as presently organized. It requires the individual to communicate by word and sign his acceptance of the political ideas it thus bespeaks. Objection to this form of communication, when coerced, is an old one, well known to the framers of the Bill of Rights.[13]

It is also to be noted that the compulsory flag salute and pledge requires affirmation of a belief and an attitude of mind. It is not clear whether the regulation contemplates that pupils forego any contrary convictions of their own and become unwilling converts to the prescribed ceremony, or whether it will be acceptable if they simulate assent by words without belief, and by a gesture barren of meaning. It is now a commonplace that censorship or suppression of expression of opinion is tolerated by our Constitution only when the expression presents a clear and present danger of action of a kind the State is empowered to prevent and punish. It would seem that involuntary affirmation could be commanded only on even more immediate and urgent grounds than silence. But here, the power of compulsion [634] is invoked without any allegation that remaining passive during a flag salute ritual creates a clear and present danger that would justify an effort even to muffle expression. To sustain the compulsory flag salute,

---

13. Early Christians were frequently persecuted for their refusal to participate in ceremonies before the statue of the emperor or other symbol of imperial authority. The story of William Tell's sentence to shoot an apple off his son's head for refusal to salute a bailiff's hat is an ancient one. 21 *Encyclopedia Britannica* (14th ed.) 911-912. The Quakers, William Penn included, suffered punishment, rather than uncover their heads in deference to any civil authority. Braithwaite, *The Beginnings of Quakerism* (1912) 200, 229-230, 232-233, 447, 451; Fox, *Quakers Courageous* (1941) 113.

we are required to say that a Bill of Rights which guards the individual's right to speak his own mind left it open to public authorities to compel him to utter what is not in his mind.

Whether the First Amendment to the Constitution will permit officials to order observance of ritual of this nature does not depend upon whether as a voluntary exercise we would think it to be good, bad or merely innocuous. Any credo of nationalism is likely to include what some disapprove or to omit what others think essential, and to give off different overtones as it takes on different accents or interpretations.[14] If official power exists to coerce acceptance of any patriotic creed, what it shall contain cannot be decided by courts, but must be largely discretionary with the ordaining authority, whose power to prescribe would no doubt include power to amend. Hence, validity of the asserted power to force an American citizen publicly to profess any statement of belief, or to engage in any ceremony of assent to one, presents questions of power that must be considered independently of any idea we may have as to the utility of the ceremony in question.

Nor does the issue, as we see it, turn on one's possession of particular religious views or the sincerity with which they are held. While religion supplies appellees' motive for enduring the discomforts of making the issue in this case, many citizens who do not share these religious views [635] hold such a compulsory rite to infringe constitutional liberty of the individual.[15] It is not necessary to inquire

---

14. For example: use of "Republic," if rendered to distinguish our government from a "democracy," or the words "one Nation," if intended to distinguish it from a "federation," open up old and bitter controversies in our political history; "liberty and justice for all," if it must be accepted as descriptive of the present order, rather than an ideal, might to some seem an overstatement.

15. Cushman, "Constitutional Law in 1939-1940," 35 *American Political Science Review* 250, 271, observes:

> All of the eloquence by which the majority extol the ceremony of flag saluting as a free expression of patriotism turns sour when used to describe the brutal compulsion which requires a sensitive and conscientious child to stultify himself in public.

For further criticism of the opinion in the *Gobitis* case by persons who do not share the faith of the Witnesses, *see* Powell, *Conscience and the Constitution, in Democracy and National Unity* (University of Chicago Press, 1941) 1; Wilkinson, "Some Aspects of the Constitutional Guarantees of Civil Liberty," 11 *Fordham Law Review* 50; Fennell, "The 'Reconstructed Court' and Religious Freedom: The *Gobitis* Case in Retrospect," 19 *New York University Law Quarterly Review* 31; Green, "Liberty under the Fourteenth

whether nonconformist beliefs will exempt from the duty to salute unless we first find power to make the salute a legal duty.

The *Gobitis* decision, however, *assumed*, as did the argument in that case and in this, that power exists in the State to impose the flag salute discipline upon school children in general. The Court only examined and rejected a claim based on religious beliefs of immunity from an unquestioned general rule.[16] The question which underlies the [636] flag salute controversy is whether such a ceremony so touching matters of opinion and political attitude may be imposed upon the individual by official authority under powers committed to any political organization under our Constitution. We examine, rather than assume existence of, this power, and, against this broader definition of issues in this case, reexamine specific grounds assigned for the *Gobitis* decision.

1. It was said that the flag salute controversy confronted the Court with

> the problem which Lincoln cast in memorable dilemma: "Must a government of necessity be too strong for the liberties of its people, or too weak to maintain its own existence?", and that the answer must be in favor of strength. *Minersville School District v. Gobitis, supra,* at 596.

We think these issues may be examined free of pressure or restraint growing out of such considerations.

Amendment," 27 *Washington University Law Quarterly* 497; 9 *International Juridical Association Bulletin* 1; 39 *Michigan Law Review* 149; 15 *St. John's Law Review* 95.

16. The opinion says

> That the flag salute is an allowable portion of a school program *for those who do not invoke conscientious scruples is surely not debatable.* But for us to insist that, *though the ceremony may be required, exceptional immunity must be given to dissidents* is to maintain that there is no basis for a legislative judgment that such an exemption might introduce elements of difficulty into the school discipline, might cast doubts in the minds of the other children which would themselves weaken the effect of the exercise.

(Italics ours.) 310 U.S. at 599-600. And, elsewhere, the question under consideration was stated,

> When does the constitutional guarantee *compel exemption* from doing what society thinks necessary for the promotion of some great common end, or from a penalty for conduct which appears dangerous to the general good?

(Italics ours.) *Id.* at 593. And again,

> ...whether school children, like the Gobitis children, must be *excused from conduct required of all the other children* in the promotion of national cohesion. . . .

(Italics ours.) *Id.* at 595.

It may be doubted whether Mr. Lincoln would have thought that the strength of government to maintain itself would be impressively vindicated by our confirming power of the State to expel a handful of children from school. Such oversimplification, so handy in political debate, often lacks the precision necessary to postulates of judicial reasoning. If validly applied to this problem, the utterance cited would resolve every issue of power in favor of those in authority, and would require us to override every liberty thought to weaken or delay execution of their policies.

Government of limited power need not be anemic government. Assurance that rights are secure tends to diminish fear and jealousy of strong government, and, by making us feel safe to live under it, makes for its better support. Without promise of a limiting Bill of Rights, it is [637] doubtful if our Constitution could have mustered enough strength to enable its ratification. To enforce those rights today is not to choose weak government over strong government. It is only to adhere as a means of strength to individual freedom of mind in preference to officially disciplined uniformity for which history indicates a disappointing and disastrous end.

The subject now before us exemplifies this principle. Free public education, if faithful to the ideal of secular instruction and political neutrality, will not be partisan or enemy of any class, creed, party, or faction. If it is to impose any ideological discipline, however, each party or denomination must seek to control, or, failing that, to weaken, the influence of the educational system. Observance of the limitations of the Constitution will not weaken government in the field appropriate for its exercise.

2. It was also considered in the *Gobitis* case that functions of educational officers in States, counties and school districts were such that to interfere with their authority "would in effect make us the school board for the country." *Id.* at 598.

The Fourteenth Amendment, as now applied to the States, protects the citizen against the State itself and all of its creatures -- Boards of Education not excepted. These have, of course, important, delicate, and highly discretionary functions, but none that they may not perform within the limits of the Bill of Rights. That they are educating the young for citizenship is reason for scrupulous protection of Constitutional freedoms of the individual, if we are not to strangle the free mind at its source and teach youth to discount important principles of our government as mere platitudes.

Such Boards are numerous, and their territorial jurisdiction often small. But small and local authority may feel less sense of responsibility to the Constitution, and agencies of publicity may be less vigilant in calling it to account. [638] The action of Congress in making flag observance voluntary[17] and respecting the conscience of the objector in a matter so vital as raising the Army[18] contrasts sharply with these local regulations in matters relatively trivial to the welfare of the nation. There are village tyrants, as well as village Hampdens, but none who acts under color of law is beyond reach of the Constitution.

3. The *Gobitis* opinion reasoned that this is a field "where courts possess no marked, and certainly no controlling, competence," that it is committed to the legislatures, as well as the courts, to guard cherished liberties, and that it is constitutionally appropriate to

> fight out the wise use of legislative authority in the forum of public opinion and before legislative assemblies, rather than to transfer such a contest to the judicial arena,

since all the "effective means of inducing political changes are left free." *Id.* at 597-598, 600.

The very purpose of a Bill of Rights was to withdraw certain subjects from the vicissitudes of political controversy, to place them beyond the reach of majorities and officials, and to establish them as legal principles to be applied by the courts. One's right to life, liberty, and property, to free speech, a free press, freedom of worship and as-

---

17. Section 7 of House Joint Resolution 359, approved December 22, 1942, 56 Stat. 1074, 36 U.S.C. (1942 Supp.) § 172, prescribes no penalties for nonconformity, but provides:

That the pledge of allegiance to the flag, "I pledge allegiance to the flag of the United States of America and to the Republic for which it stands, one Nation indivisible, with liberty and justice for all," be rendered by standing with the right hand over the heart. However, civilians will always show full respect to the flag when the pledge is given by merely standing at attention, men removing the headdress.....

18. § 5(a) of the Selective Training and Service Act of 1940, 50 U.S.C. (App.) § 307(g).

sembly, and other fundamental rights may not be submitted to vote; they depend on the outcome of no elections. [639]

In weighing arguments of the parties, it is important to distinguish between the due process clause of the Fourteenth Amendment as an instrument for transmitting the principles of the First Amendment and those cases in which it is applied for its own sake. The test of legislation which collides with the Fourteenth Amendment, because it also collides with the principles of the First, is much more definite than the test when only the Fourteenth is involved. Much of the vagueness of the due process clause disappears when the specific prohibitions of the First become its standard. The right of a State to regulate, for example, a public utility may well include, so far as the due process test is concerned, power to impose all of the restrictions which a legislature may have a "rational basis" for adopting. But freedoms of speech and of press, of assembly, and of worship may not be infringed on such slender grounds. They are susceptible of restriction only to prevent grave and immediate danger to interests which the State may lawfully protect. It is important to note that, while it is the Fourteenth Amendment which bears directly upon the State, it is the more specific limiting principles of the First Amendment that finally govern this case.

Nor does our duty to apply the Bill of Rights to assertions of official authority depend upon our possession of marked competence in the field where the invasion of rights occurs. True, the task of translating the majestic generalities of the Bill of Rights, conceived as part of the pattern of liberal government in the eighteenth century, into concrete restraints on officials dealing with the problems of the twentieth century, is one to disturb self-confidence. These principles grew in soil which also produced a philosophy that the individual was the center of society, that his liberty was attainable through mere absence of governmental restraints, and that government should be entrusted with few controls, and only the mildest supervision [640] over men's affairs. We must transplant these rights to a soil in which the *laissez-faire* concept or principle of noninterference has withered, at least as to economic affairs, and social advancements are increasingly sought through closer integration of society and through expanded and strengthened governmental controls. These changed conditions often deprive precedents of reliability, and cast us more than we would choose upon our own judgment. But we act in these matters not by authority of our competence, but by force of our commissions. We cannot, because of modest estimates of our competence in such specialties as public education, withhold the judgment that history authenticates as the function of this Court when liberty is infringed.

4. Lastly, and this is the very heart of the *Gobitis* opinion, it reasons that "National unity is the basis of national security," that the authorities have "the right to select appropriate means for its attainment," and hence reaches the conclusion that such compulsory measures toward "national unity" are constitutional. *Id.* at 595. Upon the verity of this assumption depends our answer in this case.

National unity, as an end which officials may foster by persuasion and example, is not in question. The problem is whether, under our Constitution, compulsion as here employed is a permissible means for its achievement.

Struggles to coerce uniformity of sentiment in support of some end thought essential to their time and country have been waged by many good, as well as by evil, men. Nationalism is a relatively recent phenomenon, but, at other times and places, the ends have been racial or territorial security, support of a dynasty or regime, and particular plans for saving souls. As first and moderate methods to attain unity have failed, those bent on its accomplishment must resort to an ever-increasing severity. [641] As governmental pressure toward unity becomes greater, so strife becomes more bitter as to whose unity it shall be. Probably no deeper division of our people could proceed from any provocation than from finding it necessary to choose what doctrine and whose program public educational officials shall compel youth to unite in embracing. Ultimate futility of such attempts to compel coherence is the lesson of every such effort from the Roman drive to stamp out Christianity as a disturber of its pagan unity, the Inquisition, as a means to religious and dynastic unity, the Siberian exiles as a means to Russian unity, down to the fast failing efforts of our present totalitarian enemies. Those who begin coercive elimination of dissent soon find themselves exterminating dissenters. Compulsory unification of opinion achieves only the unanimity of the graveyard.

It seems trite but necessary to say that the First Amendment to our Constitution was designed to avoid these ends by avoiding these beginnings. There is no mysticism in the American concept of the State or of the nature or origin of its authority. We set up government by consent of the governed, and the Bill of Rights denies those in power any legal opportunity to coerce that consent. Authority here is to be controlled by public opinion, not public opinion by authority.

The case is made difficult not because the principles of its decision are obscure, but because the flag involved is our own. Nevertheless, we apply the limitations of the Constitution with no fear that freedom to be intellectually and spiritually diverse or even contrary will disintegrate the social organization. To believe that patriotism will not flourish if patriotic ceremonies are voluntary and spontaneous, instead of a compulsory routine, is to make an unflattering estimate of the appeal of our institutions to free minds. We can have intellectual individualism [642] and the rich cultural diversities that we owe to exceptional minds only at the price of occasional eccentricity and abnormal attitudes. When they are so harmless to others or to the State as those we deal with here, the price is not too great. But freedom to differ is not limited to things that do not matter much. That would be a mere shadow of freedom. The test of its substance is the right to differ as to things that touch the heart of the existing order.

If there is any fixed star in our constitutional constellation, it is that no official, high or petty, can prescribe what shall be orthodox in politics, nationalism, religion, or other matters of opinion, or force citizens to confess by word or act their faith therein. If there are any circumstances which permit an exception, they do not now occur to us.[19]

We think the action of the local authorities in compelling the flag salute and pledge transcends constitutional limitations on their power, and invades the sphere of intellect and spirit which it is the purpose of

---

19. The Nation may raise armies and compel citizens to give military service. *Selective Draft Law Cases*, 245 U.S. 366. It follows, of course, that those subject to military discipline are under many duties, and may not claim many freedoms that we hold inviolable as to those in civilian life.

the First Amendment to our Constitution to reserve from all official control.

The decision of this Court in *Minersville School District v. Gobitis*, and the holdings of those few per curiam decisions which preceded and foreshadowed it, are overruled, and the judgment enjoining enforcement of the West Virginia Regulation is

Affirmed.

SUPREME COURT OF THE UNITED STATES

KEYISHIAN, ET AL., V. BOARD OF REGENTS OF THE UNIVERSITY OF THE STATE OF NEW YORK, ET AL.

(385 U.S. 589)

Argued: November 17, 1966
Decided: January 23, 1967

MR. JUSTICE BRENNAN delivered the opinion of the Court.

Appellants were members of the faculty of the privately owned and operated University of Buffalo, and became state employees when the University was merged in 1962 into the State University of New York, an institution of higher education owned and operated by the State of New York. As faculty members of the State University their continued employment was conditioned upon their compliance with a New York plan, formulated [592] partly in statutes and partly in administrative regulations,[1] which the State utilizes to prevent the appointment or retention of "subversive" persons in state employment.

Appellants Hochfield and Maud were Assistant Professors of English, appellant Keyishian an instructor in English, and appellant Garver, a lecturer in philosophy. Each of them refused to sign, as regulations then in effect required, a certificate that he was not a Communist, and that if he had ever been a Communist, he had communicated that fact to the President of the State University of New York. Each was notified that his failure to sign the certificate would require his dismissal. Keyishian's one-year-term contract was not renewed because of his failure to sign the certificate. Hochfield and Garver, whose contracts still had time to run, continue to teach, but subject to proceedings for their dismissal if the constitutionality of the New York plan is sustained. Maud has voluntarily resigned and therefore no longer has standing in this suit.

---

1. The text of the pertinent statutes and administrative regulations in effect at the time of trial appears in the Appendix to the opinion.

Appellant Starbuck was a nonfaculty library employee and part-time lecturer in English. Personnel in that classification were not required to sign a certificate but were required to answer in writing under oath the question, "Have you ever advised or taught or were you ever a member of any society or group of persons which taught or advocated the doctrine that the Government of the United States or of any political subdivisions thereof should be overthrown or overturned by force, violence or any unlawful means?" Starbuck refused to answer the question and as a result was dismissed.

Appellants brought this action for declaratory and injunctive relief, alleging that the state program violated the Federal Constitution in various respects. A three-judge [593] federal court held that the program was constitutional. 255 F.Supp. 981.[2] We noted probable jurisdiction of appellants' appeal, 384 U.S. 998. We reverse.

I.

We considered some aspects of the constitutionality of the New York plan 15 years ago in *Adler v. Board of Education*, 342 U.S. 485. That litigation arose after New York passed the Feinberg Law which added §3022 to the Education Law.[3] The Feinberg Law was enacted to implement and enforce two earlier statutes. The first was a 1917 law, now §3021 of the Education Law, under which "the utterance of any treasonable or seditious word or words or the doing of any treasonable or seditious act" is a ground for dismissal from the public school system. The second was a 1939 law which was §12-a of the Civil Service Law when *Adler* was decided and, as amended, is now §105 of that law. This law disqualifies from the civil service and from employment in the educational system any person who advocates the overthrow of government by force, violence, or any unlawful means, or publishes material advocating such overthrow or organizes or joins any society or group of persons advocating such doctrine.

---

2. The District Court initially refused to convene a three-judge court, 233 F.Supp. 752, and was reversed by the Court of Appeals for the Second Circuit. 345 F.2d 236.

3. For the history of New York loyalty-security legislation, including the Feinberg Law, see Chamberlain, *Loyalty and Legislative Action*, and that author's article in Gellhorn, *The States and Subversion*, 231.

The Feinberg Law charged the State Board of Regents with the duty of promulgating rules and regulations providing procedures for the disqualification or removal of persons in the public school system who violate the 1917 law or who are ineligible for appointment to or [594] retention in the public school system under the 1939 law. The Board of Regents was further directed to make a list, after notice and hearing, of "subversive" organizations, defined as organizations which advocate the doctrine of overthrow of government by force, violence, or any unlawful means. Finally, the Board was directed to provide in its rules and regulations that membership in any listed organization should constitute prima facie evidence of disqualification for appointment to or retention in any office or position in the public schools of the State.

The Board of Regents thereupon promulgated rules and regulations containing procedures to be followed by appointing authorities to discover persons ineligible for appointment or retention under the 1939 law, or because of violation of the 1917 law. The Board also announced its intention to list "subversive" organizations after requisite notice and hearing, and provided that membership in a listed organization after the date of its listing should be regarded as constituting prima facie evidence of disqualification, and that membership prior to listing should be presumptive evidence that membership has continued, in the absence of a showing that such membership was terminated in good faith. Under the regulations, an appointing official is forbidden to make an appointment until after he has first inquired of an applicant's former employers and other persons to ascertain whether the applicant is disqualified or ineligible for appointment. In addition, an annual inquiry must be made to determine whether an appointed employee has ceased to be qualified for retention, and a report of findings must be filed.

Adler was a declaratory judgment suit in which the Court held, in effect, that there was no constitutional infirmity in former §12-a or in the Feinberg Law on their faces and that they were capable of constitutional application. But the contention urged in this case that [595] both §3021 and §105 are unconstitutionally vague was not heard or decided. Section 3021 of the Education Law was challenged in *Adler* as unconstitutionally vague, but because the challenge had not been made in the pleadings or in the proceedings in the lower courts, this Court refused to consider it. 342 U.S., at 496. Nor was any challenge on grounds of vagueness made in Adler as to subdivisions 1 (a) and (b) of §105 of the Civil Service Law.[4] Subdivision 3 of §105 was not added until 1958. Appellants in this case timely asserted below the unconstitutionality of all these sections on grounds of vagueness and that question is now properly before us for decision. Moreover, to the extent that Adler sustained the provision of the Feinberg Law constituting membership in an organization advocating forceful overthrow of government a ground for disqualification, pertinent constitutional doctrines have since rejected the premises upon which that conclusion rested. Adler is therefore not dispositive of the constitutional issues we must decide in this case.

II.

A 1953 amendment extended the application of the Feinberg Law to personnel of any college or other institution of higher education owned and operated by the State or its subdivisions. In the same year, the Board of Regents, after notice and hearing, listed the Communist Party of the United States and of the State of New York as "subversive organizations." In 1956 each applicant for an appointment or the renewal of an appointment was required to sign the so-called "Feinberg Certificate" declaring that he had read the Regents Rules and understood that the Rules and the statutes [596] constituted terms of employment, and declaring further that he was not a member of the Communist Party, and that if he had ever been a member he had communicated that fact to the President of the State University. This was the certificate that appellants Hochfield, Maud, Keyishian, and Garver refused to sign.

In June 1965, shortly before the trial of this case, the Feinberg Certificate was rescinded and it was announced that no person then employed would be deemed ineligible for continued employment "solely" because he refused to sign the certificate. In lieu of the certificate,

---

4. The sole "vagueness" contention in *Adler* concerned the word "subversive," appearing in the preamble to and caption of §3022. 342 U.S., at 496.

it was provided that each applicant be informed before assuming his duties that the statutes, §§3021 and 3022 of the Education Law and §105 of the Civil Service Law, constituted part of his contract. He was particularly to be informed of the disqualification which flowed from membership in a listed "subversive" organization. The 1965 announcement further provides: "Should any question arise in the course of such inquiry such candidate may request... a personal interview. Refusal of a candidate to answer any question relevant to such inquiry by such officer shall be sufficient ground to refuse to make or recommend appointment." A brochure is also given new applicants. It outlines and explains briefly the legal effect of the statutes and invites any applicant who may have any question about possible disqualification to request an interview. The covering announcement concludes that "a prospective appointee who does not believe himself disqualified need take no affirmative action. No disclaimer oath is required."

The change in procedure in no wise moots appellants' constitutional questions raised in the context of their refusal to sign the now abandoned Feinberg Certificate. The substance of the statutory and regulatory complex remains and from the outset appellants' basic claim has been that they are aggrieved by its application.

[597] III.

Section 3021 requires removal for "treasonable or seditious" utterances or acts. The 1958 amendment to §105 of the Civil Service Law, now subdivision 3 of that section, added such utterances or acts as a ground for removal under that law also.[5] The same wording is used

---

5. There is no merit in the suggestion advanced by the Attorney General of New York for the first time in his brief in this Court that §3021 of the Education Law and §105, subd. 3, of the Civil Service Law are not "pertinent to our inquiry." Section 3022 of the Education Law incorporates by reference the provisions of both, thereby rendering them applicable to faculty members of all colleges and institutions of higher education. One of the reasons why the Court of Appeals ordered the convening of a three-judge court was that a substantial federal question was presented by the fact that "*Adler* . . . refused to pass upon the constitutionality of section 3021... [and that] several statutory amendments, such as Section 105 (3) of the Civil Service Law, are all subsequent to *Adler*." 345 F.2d 236, 238. The three-judge court also properly found these provisions applicable to appellants in holding them constitutional. It is significant that appellees consistently defended the constitutionality of these sections in the courts below. Moreover, the three-judge court rendered its decision upon the basis of a "Stipulation of Fact," paragraph 20 of which recites:

in both statutes -- that "the utterance of any treasonable or seditious word or words or the doing of any treasonable or seditious act or acts" shall be ground for removal. But there is a vital difference between the two laws. Section 3021 does not define the terms "treasonable or [598] seditious" as used in that section; in contrast, subdivision 3 of §105 of the Civil Service Law provides that the terms "treasonable word or act" shall mean "treason" as defined in the Penal Law and the terms "seditious word or act" shall mean "criminal anarchy" as defined in the Penal Law.

Our experience under the Sedition Act of 1798, 1 Stat. 596, taught us that dangers fatal to First Amendment freedoms inhere in the word "seditious." See *New York Times Co. v. Sullivan*, 376 U.S. 254, 273-276. And the word "treasonable," if left undefined, is no less dangerously uncertain. Thus it becomes important whether, despite the omission of a similar reference to the Penal Law in §3021, the words as used in that section are to be read as meaning only what they mean in subdivision 3 of §105. Or are they to be read more broadly and to constitute utterances or acts "seditious" and "treasonable" which would not be so regarded for the purposes of §105?

Even assuming that "treasonable" and "seditious" in §3021 and §105, subd. 3, have the same meaning, the uncertainty is hardly removed. The definition of "treasonable" in the Penal Law presents no particular problem. The difficulty centers upon the meaning of "seditious." Subdivision 3 equates the term "seditious" with "criminal anarchy" as defined in the Penal Law. Is the reference only to Penal Law §160, defining criminal anarchy as "the doctrine that organized government should be overthrown by force or violence, or by assassination of the executive head or of any of the executive officials of government, or by any unlawful means"? But that section ends with the sentence "The advocacy of such doctrine either by word of mouth or writing is a

---

"Section 3022 incorporates in full by reference and implements Section 105 of the Civil Service Law and Section 3021 of the New York State Education Law as follows: Subdivision (1) of Section 3022, as amended . . . directs the Board of Regents to adopt and enforce rules and regulations for the elimination of persons barred from employment in the public school system or any college or institution of higher education owned by the State of New York or any political subdivision thereof, by reason of violation of any of the provisions of Section 105 of the Civil Service Law or Section 3021 of the New York State Education Law."

felony." Does that sentence draw into §105, Penal Law §161, proscribing "advocacy of criminal anarchy"? If so, the [599] possible scope of "seditious" utterances or acts has virtually no limit. For under Penal Law §161, one commits the felony of advocating criminal anarchy if he ". . . publicly displays any book . . . containing or advocating, advising or teaching the doctrine that organized government should be overthrown by force, violence or any unlawful means."[6] Does the teacher who carries a copy of the Communist Manifesto on a public street thereby advocate criminal anarchy? It is no answer to say that the statute would not be applied in such a case. We cannot gainsay the potential effect of this obscure wording on "those with a conscientious and scrupulous regard for such undertakings." *Baggett v. Bullitt,* 377 U.S. 360, 374. Even were it certain that the definition referred to in §105 was solely Penal Law §160, the scope of §105 still remains indefinite. The teacher cannot know the extent, if any, to which a "seditious" utterance must transcend mere statement about abstract doctrine, the extent to which it must be intended to and tend to indoctrinate or incite to action in furtherance of the defined doctrine. The crucial consideration is that no teacher can know just where the line is drawn between "seditious" and nonseditious utterances and acts.

Other provisions of §105 also have the same defect of vagueness. Subdivision 1 (a) of §105 bars employment of any person who "by word of mouth or writing wilfully and deliberately advocates, advises or teaches the doctrine" of forceful overthrow of government. This provision is plainly susceptible of sweeping and improper application. It may well prohibit the employment of one who merely advocates the doctrine in the abstract without any attempt to indoctrinate others, or incite [600] others to action in furtherance of unlawful aims.[7] See

---

6. Penal Law §§160-161 are to be replaced effective September 1, 1967, by a single provision entitled "criminal advocacy."

7. The New York State Legislative Committee on Public Employee Security Procedures, in describing this provision, noted:

"In disqualifying for employment those who advocate or teach the 'doctrine' of the violent overthrow of government, [§105] is to be distinguished from the language of the Smith Act (18 U. S. C. §§371, 2385), which has been construed by the Supreme Court to make it criminal to incite to 'action' for the forcible overthrow of government, but not to teach the 'abstract doctrine' of such forcible overthrow. *Yates v. United States,* 354 U.S. 298 (1957)." 1958 N. Y. State Legis. Annual 70, n. 1.

Herndon v. Lowry, 301 U.S. 242; *Yates v. United States,* 354 U.S. 298; *Noto v. United States,* 367 U.S. 290; *Scales v. United States,* 367 U.S. 203. And in prohibiting "advising" the "doctrine" of unlawful overthrow does the statute prohibit mere "advising" of the existence of the doctrine, or advising another to support the doctrine? Since "advocacy" of the doctrine of forceful overthrow is separately prohibited, need the person "teaching" or "advising" this doctrine himself "advocate" it? Does the teacher who informs his class about the precepts of Marxism or the Declaration of Independence violate this prohibition?

Similar uncertainty arises as to the application of subdivision 1 (b) of §105. That subsection requires the disqualification of an employee involved with the distribution of written material "containing or advocating, advising or teaching the doctrine" of forceful overthrow, and who himself "advocates, advises, teaches, or embraces the duty, necessity or propriety of adopting the doctrine contained therein." Here again, mere advocacy of abstract doctrine is apparently included.[8] And does [601] the prohibition of distribution of matter "containing" the doctrine bar histories of the evolution of Marxist doctrine or tracing the background of the French, American, or Russian revolutions? The additional requirement, that the person participating in distribution of the material be one who "advocates, advises, teaches, or embraces the duty, necessity or propriety of adopting the doctrine" of forceful overthrow, does not alleviate the uncertainty in the scope of the section, but exacerbates it. Like the language of §105, subd. 1 (a), this language may reasonably be construed to cover mere expression of belief. For example, does the university librarian who recommends the reading of such materials thereby "advocate...the...propriety of adopting the doctrine contained therein"?

We do not have the benefit of a judicial gloss by the New York courts enlightening us as to the scope of this complicated plan.[9] In

8.Compare the Smith Act, 18 U. S. C. §2385, which punishes one who "prints, publishes, edits, issues, circulates, sells, distributes, or publicly displays any written or printed matter advocating, advising, or teaching the duty, necessity, desirability, or propriety of" unlawful overthrow, provided he is shown to have an "intent to cause the overthrow or destruction of any such government."

9.This is not a case where abstention pending state court interpretation would be appropriate, *Baggett v. Bullitt, supra,* at 375-379; *Dombrowski v. Pfister,* 380 U.S. 479, 489-490.

light of the intricate administrative machinery for its enforcement, this is not surprising. The very intricacy of the plan and the uncertainty as to the scope of its proscriptions make it a highly efficient *in terrorem* mechanism. It would be a bold teacher who would not stay as far as possible from utterances or acts which might jeopardize his living by enmeshing him in this intricate machinery. The uncertainty as to the utterances and acts proscribed increases that caution in "those who believe the written law means what it says." *Baggett v. Bullitt, supra*, at 374. The result must be to stifle "that free play of the spirit which all teachers ought especially to cultivate and practice...."[10] That probability is enhanced by the provisions requiring an [602] annual review of every teacher to determine whether any utterance or act of his, inside the classroom or out, came within the sanctions of the laws. For a memorandum warns employees that under the statutes "subversive" activities may take the form of "the writing of articles, the distribution of pamphlets, the endorsement of speeches made or articles written or acts performed by others," and reminds them "that it is a primary duty of the school authorities in each school district to take positive action to eliminate from the school system any teacher in whose case there is evidence that he is guilty of subversive activity. School authorities are under obligation to proceed immediately and conclusively in every such case."

There can be no doubt of the legitimacy of New York's interest in protecting its education system from subversion. But "even though the governmental purpose be legitimate and substantial, that purpose cannot be pursued by means that broadly stifle fundamental personal liberties when the end can be more narrowly achieved." *Shelton v. Tucker*, 364 U.S. 479, 488. The principle is not inapplicable because the legislation is aimed at keeping subversives out of the teaching ranks. In *De Jonge v. Oregon*, 299 U.S. 353, 365, the Court said:

> The greater the importance of safeguarding the community from incitements to the overthrow of our institutions by force and violence, the more imperative is the need to preserve inviolate the constitutional rights of free speech, free press and free assembly in order to maintain the opportunity for free political discussion, to the end that government may be responsive to the will of the people and that changes, if desired, may be obtained by

---

10. *Wieman v. Updegraff*, 344 U.S. 183, 195 (Frankfurter, J., concurring).

peaceful means. Therein lies the security of the Republic, the very foundation of constitutional government.

[603] Our Nation is deeply committed to safeguarding academic freedom, which is of transcendent value to all of us and not merely to the teachers concerned. That freedom is therefore a special concern of the First Amendment, which does not tolerate laws that cast a pall of orthodoxy over the classroom. "The vigilant protection of constitutional freedoms is nowhere more vital than in the community of American schools." *Shelton v. Tucker, supra,* at 487. The classroom is peculiarly the "marketplace of ideas." The Nation's future depends upon leaders trained through wide exposure to that robust exchange of ideas which discovers truth "out of a multitude of tongues, [rather] than through any kind of authoritative selection." *United States v. Associated Press,* 52 F.Supp. 362, 372. In *Sweezy v. New Hampshire,* 354 U.S. 234, 250, we said:

> The essentiality of freedom in the community of American universities is almost self-evident. No one should underestimate the vital role in a democracy that is played by those who guide and train our youth. To impose any strait jacket upon the intellectual leaders in our colleges and universities would imperil the future of our Nation. No field of education is so thoroughly comprehended by man that new discoveries cannot yet be made. Particularly is that true in the social sciences, where few, if any, principles are accepted as absolutes. Scholarship cannot flourish in an atmosphere of suspicion and distrust. Teachers and students must always remain free to inquire, to study and to evaluate, to gain new maturity and understanding; otherwise our civilization will stagnate and die.

We emphasize once again that "precision of regulation must be the touchstone in an area so closely touching our most precious freedoms," *N. A. A. C. P. v. Button,* [604] 371 U.S. 415, 438; "for standards of permissible statutory vagueness are strict in the area of free expression.... Because First Amendment freedoms need breathing space to survive, government may regulate in the area only with narrow specificity." *Id.,* at 432-433. New York's complicated and intricate scheme plainly violates that standard. When one must guess what conduct or utterance may lose him his position, one necessarily will "steer far wider of the unlawful zone...." *Speiser v. Randall,* 357 U.S. 513, 526. For "the threat of sanctions may deter...almost as potently as the actual application of sanctions." *N. A. A. C. P. v. Button, supra,* at 433. The danger of that chilling effect upon the exercise of vital First Amendment rights must be guarded against by sensitive tools which clearly inform teachers what is being proscribed. See *Stromberg v. California*, 283 U.S. 359, 369; *Cramp v. Board of Public Instruction*, 368 U.S. 278; *Baggett v. Bullitt, supra.*

The regulatory maze created by New York is wholly lacking in "terms susceptible of objective measurement." *Cramp v. Board of Public Instruction, supra*, at 286. It has the quality of "extraordinary ambiguity" found to be fatal to the oaths considered in *Cramp* and *Baggett v. Bullitt*. "Men of common intelligence must necessarily guess at its meaning and differ as to its application...." *Baggett v. Bullitt, supra*, at 367. Vagueness of wording is aggravated by prolixity and profusion of statutes, regulations, and administrative machinery, and by manifold cross-references to interrelated enactments and rules.

We therefore hold that §3021 of the Education Law and subdivisions 1 (a), 1 (b) and 3 of §105 of the Civil Service Law as implemented by the machinery created pursuant to §3022 of the Education Law are unconstitutional.

[605] IV.

Appellants have also challenged the constitutionality of the discrete provisions of subdivision 1 (c) of §105 and subdivision 2 of the Feinberg Law, which make Communist Party membership, as such, prima facie evidence of disqualification. The provision was added to subdivision 1 (c) of §105 in 1958 after the Board of Regents, following notice and hearing, listed the Communist Party of the United States and the Communist Party of the State of New York as "subversive" organizations. Subdivision 2 of the Feinberg Law was, however, before the Court in *Adler* and its constitutionality was sustained. But constitutional doctrine which has emerged since that decision has rejected its major premise. That premise was that public employment, including academic employment, may be conditioned upon the surrender of constitutional rights which could not be abridged by direct government action. Teachers, the Court said in *Adler*, "may work for the school system upon the reasonable terms laid down by the proper authorities of New York. If they do not choose to work on such terms, they are at liberty to retain their beliefs and associations and go elsewhere." 342 U.S., at 492. The Court also stated that a teacher denied employment because of membership in a listed organization "is not thereby denied the right of free speech and assembly. His freedom of choice between membership in the organization and employment in the school system might be limited, but not his freedom of speech or assembly, except in the remote sense that limitation is inherent in every choice." *Id.*, at 493.

However, the Court of Appeals for the Second Circuit correctly said in an earlier stage of this case, ". . . the theory that public employment which may be denied altogether may be subjected to any conditions, regardless [606] of how unreasonable, has been uniformly rejected." *Keyishian v. Board of Regents*, 345 F.2d 236, 239. Indeed, that theory was expressly rejected in a series of decisions following *Adler*. See *Wieman v. Updegraff*, 344 U.S. 183; *Slochower v. Board of Education*, 350 U.S. 551; *Cramp v. Board of Public Instruction, supra*; *Baggett v. Bullitt, supra*; *Shelton v. Tucker, supra*; *Speiser v. Randall, supra*; see also *Schware v. Board of Bar Examiners*, 353 U.S. 232; *Torcaso v. Watkins*, 367 U.S. 488. In *Sherbert v. Verner*, 374 U.S. 398, 404, we said: "It is too late in the day to doubt that the liberties of religion and expression may be infringed by the denial of or placing of conditions upon a benefit or privilege."

We proceed then to the question of the validity of the provisions of subdivision 1 (c) of §105 and subdivision 2 of §3022, barring employment to members of listed organizations. Here again constitutional doctrine has developed since *Adler*. Mere knowing membership without a specific intent to further the unlawful aims of an organization is not a constitutionally adequate basis for exclusion from such positions as those held by appellants.

In *Elfbrandt v. Russell*, 384 U.S. 11, we said, "Those who join an organization but do not share its unlawful purposes and who do not participate in its unlawful activities surely pose no threat, either as citizens or as public employees." *Id.*, at 17. We there struck down a statutorily required oath binding the state employee not to become a member of the Communist Party with knowledge of its unlawful purpose, on threat of discharge and perjury prosecution if the oath were violated. We found that "any lingering doubt that proscription of mere knowing membership, without any showing of 'specific intent,' would run afoul of the Constitution was set at rest by our decision in *Aptheker v. Secretary of State*, 378 U.S. 500." *Elfbrandt v. Russell, supra*, at 16. In *Aptheker* we held that Party membership, without knowledge [607] of the Party's unlawful purposes and specific intent to further its unlawful aims, could not constitutionally warrant deprivation of the right to travel abroad. As we said in *Schneiderman v. United States*, 320 U.S. 118, 136, "Under our traditions beliefs are personal and not a matter of mere association, and...men in adhering to a political party or other organization...do not subscribe unqualifiedly to all of its platforms or asserted principles." "A law which applies to membership without the 'specific intent' to further the illegal aims of the organization infringes unnecessarily on protected freedoms. It rests on the doctrine of 'guilt by association' which has no place here." *Elfbrandt, supra*, at 19. Thus mere Party membership, even with knowledge of the Party's unlawful goals, cannot suffice to justify criminal punishment, see *Scales v. United States*, 367 U.S. 203; *Noto v. United States*, 367 U.S. 290; *Yates v. United States*, 354 U.S. 298;[11] nor may it warrant a finding of moral unfitness justifying disbarment. *Schware v. Board of Bar Examiners*, 353 U.S. 232.

These limitations clearly apply to a provision, like §105, subd. 1(c), which blankets all state employees, regardless of the "sensitivity" of their positions. But even the Feinberg Law provision, applicable primarily to activities of teachers, who have captive audiences of young minds, are subject to these limitations in favor of freedom of expression and association; the stifling effect on the academic mind from curtailing freedom of association in such manner is manifest, and has been documented in recent studies.[12] *Elfbrandt* and *Aptheker* state the

---

11. Whether or not loss of public employment constitutes "punishment," cf. *United States v. Lovett*, 328 U.S. 303, there can be no doubt that the repressive impact of the threat of discharge will be no less direct or substantial.

12. See Lazarsfeld & Thielens, *The Academic Mind*, 92-112, 192-217; Biddle, *The Fear of Freedom* 155 et seq.; Jahoda & Cook, "Security Measures and Freedom of Thought: An Exploratory Study of the Impact of Loyalty and Security Programs, "61 *Yale L. J.* 295 (1952). See generally, MacIver, *Academic Freedom in Our Time*; Hullfish, *Educational Freedom*

[608] governing standard: legislation which sanctions membership unaccompanied by specific intent to further the unlawful goals of the organization or which is not active membership violates constitutional limitations.

Measured against this standard, both Civil Service Law §105, subd. 1 (c), and Education Law §3022, subd. 2, sweep overbroadly into association which may not be proscribed. The presumption of disqualification arising from proof of mere membership may be rebutted, but only by (a) a denial of membership, (b) a denial that the organization advocates the overthrow of government by force, or (c) a denial that the teacher has knowledge of such advocacy. *Lederman v. Board of Education*, 276 App. Div. 527, 96 N. Y. S. 2d 466, aff'd, 301 N. Y. 476, 95 N. E. 2d 806.[13] Thus proof of nonactive membership or a showing of the absence of intent to further unlawful aims will not rebut the presumption and defeat dismissal. This is emphasized in official administrative interpretations. For example, it is said in a letter addressed to prospective appointees by the President of the State University, "You will note that...both the Law and regulations are very specifically directed toward the elimination and nonappointment of 'Communists' from or to our teaching ranks...." The Feinberg Certificate was even more explicit: "Anyone who is a [609] member of the Communist Party or of any organization that advocates the violent overthrow of the Government of the United States or of the State of New York or any political subdivision thereof cannot be employed by the State University." (Emphasis supplied.) This official administrative interpretation is supported by the legislative preamble to the Feinberg Law, §1, in which the legislature concludes as a result of its findings that "it is essential that the laws prohibiting persons who are members of subversive groups, such as the communist party and its affiliated organizations, from obtaining or retaining employment in the public schools, be rigorously enforced." (Emphasis supplied.)

---

in an Age of Anxiety; Konvitz, *Expanding Liberties* 86-108; Morris, "Academic Freedom and Loyalty Oaths, "28 *Law & Contemp. Prob.* 487 (1963).

13, In light of our disposition, we need not consider appellants' contention that the burden placed on the employee of coming forward with substantial rebutting evidence upon proof of membership in a listed organization is constitutionally impermissible. Compare *Speiser v. Randall*, 357 U.S. 513.

Thus §105, subd. 1 (c), and §3022, subd. 2, suffer from impermissible "overbreadth." *Elfbrandt v. Russell, supra,* at 19; *Aptheker v. Secretary of State, supra; N. A. A. C. P. v. Button, supra; Saia v. New York,* 334 U.S. 558; *Schneider v. State,* 308 U.S. 147; *Lovell v. Griffin,* 303 U.S. 444; cf. *Hague v. C. I. O.,* 307 U.S. 496, 515-516; see generally *Dombrowski v. Pfister,* 380 U.S. 479, 486. They seek to bar employment both for association which legitimately may be proscribed and for association which may not be proscribed consistently with First Amendment rights. Where statutes have an overbroad sweep, just as where they are vague, "the hazard of loss or substantial impairment of those precious rights may be critical," *Dombrowski v. Pfister, supra,* at 486, since those covered by the statute are bound to limit their behavior to that which is unquestionably safe. As we said in *Shelton v. Tucker, supra,* at 488, "The breadth of legislative abridgment must be viewed in the light of less drastic means for achieving the same basic purpose."

We therefore hold that Civil Service Law §105, subd. 1 (c), and Education Law §3022, subd. 2, are invalid insofar as they proscribe mere knowing membership [610] without any showing of specific intent to further the unlawful aims of the Communist Party of the United States or of the State of New York.

The judgment of the District Court is reversed and the case is remanded for further proceedings consistent with this opinion.

Reversed and remanded.

Selected Bibliography

Burpo, Todd, and Lynn Vincent. *Heaven Is for Real: A Little Boy's Astounding Story of His Trip to Heaven and Back.* Nashville, Tenn.: Thomas Nelson, 2010.

Commission on Religion and Belief in British Public Life. *Living with Difference: Community, Diversity, and the Common Good.* Cambridge: The Woolf Institute, 2015.

Cohen, Andrew Jason. "What Toleration Is." *Ethics* 115 (1) (2004), 68–95.

Fish, Stanley. "Mission Impossible: Settling the Just Bounds Between Church and State." *Columbia Law Review* 97 (8) (1997), 2255–2333.

_____. "Stepping on Jesus." *New York Times*, April 15, 2013. http://opinionator.blogs.nytimes.com/2013/04/15/stepping-on-jesus.

Fletcher, George. "The Instability of Tolerance." In *Toleration: An Elusive Virtue*, edited by David Heyd, 158-172. Princeton: Princeton University Press, 1996.

Forst, Rainer. *Toleration in Conflict: Past and Present.* Cambridge: Cambridge University Press, 2013.

Galeotti, Anna Elisabetta. *Toleration as Recognition.* Cambridge: Cambridge University Press, 2002.

Heyd, David. "Is toleration a political virtue?" In *Toleration and its Limits*, edited by Melissa S. Williams and Jeremy Waldron, 171–194. New York: New York University Press, 2008.

Hurd, Elizabeth. *Beyond Religious Freedom.* Princeton: Princeton University Press, 2015.

Jaschik, Scott. "I was doing my job." *Inside Higher Ed*, April 1 2013. https://www.insidehighered.com/news/2013/04/01/interview-professor-center-jesus-debate-florida-atlantic.

Jones, Peter. "Beliefs and Identities." In *Toleration, Identity, and Difference*, edited by John Horton and Susan Mendus, 65-86. New York: St. Martin's Press, 1999.

Johnson, Dominic D.P., and Zoey Reeve. "The Virtues of Intolerance: Is Religion an Adaptation for War?" In *Religion, Intolerance, and Conflict: A Scientific and Conceptual Investigation*, edited by Steve Clarke, Russell Powell, and Julian Savulescu, 67-87. Oxford: Oxford University Press, 2013.

Keyishian v. Board of Regents of the University of the State of New York, 385 U.S. 589 (1967).

Kruth, Susan. "Cameron U. Sued After Prohibiting Student from Distributing Flyers." TheFire.org, May 23, 2014. https://www.thefire.org/cameron-u-sued-after-prohibiting-student-from-distributing-flyers/.

Leiter, Brian. *Why Tolerate Religion?* Princeton: Princeton University Press, 2014.

Logue, Josh. "Defining Intolerance." *Inside Higher Ed*, March 16, 2016. https://www.insidehighered.com/news/2016/03/16/u-california-considers-revised-intolerance-policy.

MacIntyre, Alasdair. *Three Rival Versions of Moral Enquiry.* Notre Dame: University of Notre Dame Press, 1990.

McCloskey, Deirdre. *The Rhetoric of Economics.* Madison, Wisc.: University of Wisconsin Press, 1985.

Menand, Louis. *The Marketplace of Ideas: Reform and Resistance in the American University* (Issues of Our Time). New York: W. W. Norton & Company, 2010.

Mendus, Susan, ed. *Justifying Toleration: Conceptual and Historical Perspectives.* Cambridge: Cambridge University Press, 2009.

Nussbaum, Martha C. *The New Religious Intolerance: Overcoming the Politics of Fear in an Anxious Age.* Cambridge, Mass.: Harvard University Press, 2012.

_____. *Liberty of Conscience: In Defense of America's Tradition of Religious Equality.* New York: Basic Books, 2008.

Perry, John, and Nigel Biggar, "Religion and intolerance: A critical commentary," in Steve Clarke, Russell Powell, and Julian Savulescu, eds., *Religion, Intolerance, and Conflict: A Scientific and Conceptual Investigation*, 253–265. Oxford: Oxford University Press, 2013.

Rorty, Richard. "Pragmatism, Relativism, and Irrationalism." In *Consequences of Pragmatism*, 160-175. Minneapolis: University of Minnesota Press, 1982.

Said, Edward. *Reflections on Exile and Other Essays.* Cambridge, Mass.: Harvard University Press, 2000.

Thompson, Robert J. *Beyond Reason and Tolerance: The Purpose and Practice of Higher Education.* New York: Oxford University Press, 2014.

Trigg, Roger. *Religious Diversity.* Cambridge: Cambridge University Press, 2014.

West Virginia State Board of Education v. Barnette, 319 U.S. 624 (1943).

Westacott, Emrys. *The Virtues of Our Vices.* Princeton: Princeton University Press, 2011.

Williams, Bernard. "Toleration: An Impossible Virtue?" In *Toleration: An Elusive Virtue*, edited by David Heyd, 18-27. Princeton: Princeton University Press, 1996.

.